Divorce and Separation

Dr Mary Welstead is Visiting Professor in Family Law at the University of Buckingham and Visiting Fellow at the Child Advocacy Program, Harvard Law School. She studied law at Cambridge University and has taught family law in a number of English universities over the past 24 years, as well as writing extensively on the topic for many different audiences. She is the joint author of a very readable textbook, *Family Law* (second edition, Oxford University Press, 2008); the third edition will be published in March 2011. Between 2003 and 2008, she helped to set up a new university in Sarajevo. Mary has three children and numerous grandchildren, and lives with her husband in Massachusetts and Oxfordshire. They have all helped to centre her attention on the importance and complications of family life.

Overcoming Common Problems Series

Selected titles

A full list of titles is available from Sheldon Press,
36 Causton Street, London SW1P 4ST and on our website at
www.sheldonpress.co.uk

Overcoming Common Problems

Divorce and Separation
A legal guide for all couples

DR MARY WELSTEAD

First published in Great Britain in 2010

Sheldon Press
36 Causton Street
London SW1P 4ST
www.sheldonpress.co.uk

British Library Cataloguing-in-Publication Data
A catalogue record for this book is available from the British Library

ISBN 978-1-84709-092-8

1 3 5 7 9 10 8 6 4 2

Typeset by Fakenham Photosetting Ltd, Fakenham, Norfolk
Printed in Great Britain by Ashford Colour Press

Produced on paper from sustainable forests

Contents

Preface

In 2009 with the economy in decline, family lawyers saw an increase in the number of clients seeking legal advice to end their relationships. One of them remarked, 'When money flies out of the window, love walks out of the door. In good times money papers over the cracks in a relationship; in bad times fault lines become law suits.' Relate, an organization which provides relationship counselling, also experienced an increase in the number of troubled couples contacting them for advice.

Even in good economic times, almost 50 per cent of all marriages end in divorce in the UK. As yet, it is too early to say whether civil partnerships will follow a similar pattern; they have only been in existence since 2005 when the Civil Partnership Act 2004 came into effect.

This book is for all of you, whether spouses or civil partners, who are experiencing problems in your relationships. It aims to guide you through the breakdown of your relationship, and the legal process necessary to end it if that is what you decide to do, and forward to the new life which, I assure you, is waiting for you, although you may not necessarily believe it now.

The book may also prove useful to counsellors, therapists and social workers working with clients whose relationships are in difficulties, as well as to the general reader.

A glossary of legal terms and a list of useful addresses and suggestions for further reading will be found at the end of the book.

It is hard to dedicate a book on relationship breakdown to any one person so I will not do so. Instead I would like to thank all those who have sought my advice, and whose courage and determination to survive have taught me so much about the personal process of relationship breakdown. I can only admire them; they know who they are.

Finally, I must thank Jeremy for his patient reading of the draft of the book to make sure that non-lawyers could understand it, not an easy task for a beloved partner to so willingly undertake.

The law is stated as at 1 January 2010.

Note to the reader

The contents of this book are intended to provide general guidance and information, and are not intended to replace individual legal or other advice from a qualified professional. While all reasonable efforts have been made to ensure that the information provided is accurate as of 1 January 2010, it does not constitute legal or professional advice and its accuracy is not guaranteed. No responsibility can be accepted by the author or publisher for any use made of the information presented in this book. Always consult a professional adviser for advice, which may apply to the particular circumstances of your case.

Introduction

When couples marry or become civil partners, most of them happily agree to share their lives with each other in a spirit of mutual trust and with an expectation that their relationship will last. They do not normally prepare for the possibility that it might break down.

Whether you are married or a civil partner, you too probably began your relationship full of hopes and dreams with the love of your life. It probably did not cross your mind that one day your relationship might become one of the many which fail. So when you are forced to confront the fact that your relationship is in serious difficulty, you are likely to be at a loss as to what to do next.

The realization that your relationship appears to be failing may have happened very suddenly. Perhaps, to your immense surprise, your partner has announced that he or she is having an affair or no longer loves you, and wants to leave. Alternatively, your awareness that all is not well may have been slowly developing over a long time before the stage is reached where you can no longer ignore it.

Whichever category you fall into, you are likely to feel a mixture of emotions. You may be distressed, confused, worried, agitated, shocked, afraid, relieved or even exhilarated if you are in the grip of a new love affair. When you are in such a state of turmoil, you may have very little sense of what is happening to you. Everything feels a little unreal. You have no idea what to do. Most of you have not been here before. Anthony Julius, the lawyer who acted for the Princess of Wales in her divorce, said to her when she asked him if he would represent her: 'I'm not a divorce lawyer; if I acted for you it would be my first divorce case.' To which the Princess wryly replied: 'It's my first divorce.'

One of the best ways for a beginner is to try to understand as much as possible about your relationship breakdown, and the law and legal process related to ending relationships. This knowledge may help you through the turmoil to a new place where you will feel stronger and calmer and ready to face your future.

When you were planning your wedding or civil partnership, you probably found yourself happily wading through vast amounts of information and advice on how to organize the most perfect day of your life. When it comes to relationship breakdown, there is also plenty of information and advice both in the media and scattered around an ever-growing number of websites. Some of the advice is helpful and some of the information is excellent and accurate, but what has been lacking up to now is a source of advice and information readily accessible in one place which will help you deal with the realities of relationship breakdown, and the legal ending of your relationship if that is what you decide to do.

This book aims to fill that gap. It is a practical guide which does not skate over the difficulties of leaving your relationship and legally ending it. I do not try to dissuade you from using the services of a lawyer. In complex cases, I actually urge you to do so.

If you decide to consult a lawyer, you may find it helpful to read this book first. It will give you a better understanding of the law and the legal process you will have to go through. This will help to empower you, as well as reduce time spent in your lawyer's office. Lawyers' fees are calculated by the hour. You will be charged for every meeting, telephone call, email and letter. Extensive questioning, or weeping (and everyone is likely to weep, at least a little, in these circumstances), in your lawyer's office will lead to expensive bills.

If you decide that you would rather go it alone and manage the legal process of ending your relationship yourself, which for many people (although not all) is perfectly possible, this book will help guide you through its various stages.

The book is organized in a way that will take you through those early days, where you may want to stay in bed sobbing quietly under your duvet, or where you vacillate between euphoria that the miseries of your relationship will soon be at an end and panic about the uncertainty of life without your current partner. It moves on to explain in straightforward language the requirements you must meet to legally end your relationship, followed by an account of how to redistribute your property and other assets and make suitable arrangements for your children. It then guides you through the legal process of obtaining decrees of divorce, separation or nullity for spouses, or dissolution, separation or nullity orders for civil partners. The book ends on an optimistic note with a discussion of how to face the new life which lies ahead of you.

The law discussed in the book relates only to England and Wales (referred to as the jurisdiction); they share the same legal system. Scotland and Northern Ireland have different laws and these jurisdictions require their own specialist legal guide.

Since 2005, civil partners have been given the same rights as married couples. The law relating to the ending of civil partnerships is virtually identical to that for ending marriages, although the names given to the legal processes are not. The similarities make it possible for both relationships to be considered alongside each other throughout the book. Where there is any significant difference between the law's treatment of spouses and its treatment of civil partners, I have highlighted it for you. For the most part, I have used the term 'partner' to refer to both spouses and civil partners. In the small number of circumstances where the law treats them differently, I have used the terms 'spouses' or 'husbands and wives', and 'civil partners'. Couples who are neither married nor in civil partnerships are referred to as 'cohabitants'.

At the end of the book, in the 'Useful addresses' and 'Further reading' sections, you will find a list of resources which may prove helpful, particularly if you are aiming to go through the legal process without the help of a lawyer. You will also find a Glossary of legal terms.

Whether you march bravely or stagger wearily through relationship breakdown towards its legal end and the beginning of your new life, you will spend a lot of time grappling with the complexities of human emotions and behaviour. At the same time, you will also have to try to understand the legal process with its unfamiliar language. My hope is that this book will help you on your journey, and I wish you well.

1

My relationship is in difficulties

My relationship is in difficulties – what shall I do?

Once you have acknowledged that your relationship is in difficulties, there is an enormous temptation to rush around frenetically or simply to bury your head under your duvet. Dashing around in a state of fear, confusion, excitement or guilt may occupy you and take your mind off your problems but it will achieve nothing. Lurking under the duvet in a state of depression and inactivity is no better. Both these temptations should be resisted resolutely. Your task now is to manage the problem facing you, and minimize the damage to yourself and your family.

You need a breathing space, a time to think and absorb what has happened, or is happening, to you and your partner. Although you may be acutely aware that life as you knew it is over, it does not necessarily mean that your relationship is.

What has happened to us?

Perhaps the excitement of falling in love has been replaced by the humdrum nature of everyday life. Maybe you fear that you never fell in love with your partner and that you have missed out on one of life's important experiences. The demands of children, the stress of work

1

and financial worries or the care of elderly parents may have left you little time to spend together, and you feel overwhelmed, depressed or ignored. You may be confronting a violent abusive relationship or a partner's illness, disability or addictive behaviour. You may be contemplating having, or have already started, an affair which makes you feel exhilarated at the thought of a new relationship but guilty because you have betrayed your partner. Perhaps you thought that your relationship was perfectly all right when, to your surprise and amazement, your partner has suddenly made it clear that this is not so.

Pause for a while

Pause for a while, and read the rest of this book before you take any decisive action about the future of your relationship, something you might later regret. Remember that there are many paths through the inevitable chaos of relationship breakdown, and no one path is suited to everyone. You need to find a route which is appropriate for you, given your personality, your own particular value system and your view of life and relationships.

You are likely to find yourself bombarded with advice from well-meaning friends and family, regardless of their own experiences of relationship breakdown. Remind yourself that they all have their own agendas, which may be very different from yours, and consider their advice cautiously.

There will be times when everything seems to be a total muddle and you feel incapable of making any decisions. At such times, believe in yourself and continually remind yourself that you will find a way through the confusion, but it may not be as clear-cut or straightforward a path as you had hoped.

The only exception to any of the above advice is if you find yourself in a violent relationship. Then, it is of the utmost importance that you take immediate action and do everything possible to protect yourself and your children (see Chapter 2 for more information on what to do in the case of a violent relationship).

Communicate with your partner

Your partner is not a clairvoyant. Unless you have discussed your concerns, you will have no idea how he or she feels about the relationship, or whether he or she shares your concerns. It can come as a considerable shock to one partner who feels content within a relationship to learn that the other is deeply unhappy. Do everything within your power to communicate honestly at this point; it is almost impossible to make progress if you do not.

Even if you are certain that you want to leave, you owe it to your partner to spend some time discussing what has gone wrong before you take any irrevocable step.

If you are contemplating a new relationship, it is usually better first to explore what has gone wrong with your present one. Humans are notorious for repeating negative behaviour if they do not question why. The exploration may help you to find a new way of approaching your present relationship and make you decide to stay with your partner. If you do decide to leave, any new relationship will have a much better chance of success. You may, of course, find that your partner does not wish to help you in this task and risk redundancy if you decide to pursue the new relationship.

Choosing the time to talk

Once you have decided to talk to your partner, choose the time with care and sensitivity. Do not do as one man did: he took his wife to Paris and, over a sumptuous dinner in a romantic restaurant, told her that he was having an affair and wanted a divorce. His explanation for choosing to tell her in this way was that he thought it would lessen the hurt for her!

Once you have raised the matter with your partner, try to arrange an appropriate time, or times, for further discussion when you know that you will both be free to talk about your problems without disturbance. If you have children, try to arrange for them to stay with friends or family for the night. It is never a good idea to talk when you are over-whelmed with pressure from work or any other stressful situation. Do not, for instance, wade into emotional discussions the moment you or your partner walk in through the door after a long day at work. It may not always be possible to avoid discussions when one party is stressed if the stress itself is the cause of the breakdown of the relationship. The problems will have to be addressed regardless.

Even at times of relationship turmoil, there may be happy moments. Don't destroy these by indulging in acrimonious discussions. Sometimes, it is these brief moments of happiness which act as the trigger for rescuing the relationship.

Be prepared for the reaction

When you voice your concerns about your relationship, particularly for the first time, be aware that your partner may react in any number of ways. He or she may be hysterical, angry, lethargic, seemingly uncaring or even hugely relieved that the matter has at last been brought out into the open.

If you suspect that there might be a violent reaction, you must consider carefully what arrangements to make to ensure your protection. Perhaps alert a friend, on whom you can rely, to be at hand if you need help. If your partner does react violently, remove yourself and any children to a place of safety immediately.

What to talk about

There are no precise rules on what you should talk about. Often talking about some apparently trivial or irrelevant matter can lead to the most intense and helpful discussions about more important issues.

It may be of help to hear what other couples have talked about before reaching a decision to remain together or part. You might like to add your own questions to the following list:

- Do we still love and care about each other?
- Why does either of us feel resentful about the relationship?
- What would we have to change to be willing to stay together?
- Is such a change realistically possible?
- What do we like about our relationship, if anything?
- Can I forgive your affair, alcoholism, drug addiction or other unacceptable conduct? Is it possible for there to be a long-term change in this behaviour?
- Can you forgive me for what I have done?
- Why has our sexual relationship ended? Can it be revived? If not, are we prepared to live without it and show our love for each other in other ways?
- Why do you spend more time with friends or colleagues, working, playing or watching sport, than you do with me?
- I am concerned about my own behaviour; am I able to change it? Can you help me to do so?
- What can we do to make life more enjoyable?
- What interests do we share?
- I am stressed out with caring for the children on my own; what can you do to help?
- I am having problems dealing with elderly parents; what can we do to make it easier?
- We have enormous financial problems; what can we do to address these?

- Is there anything we can do to help me deal with your illness or disability?
- What would the practical and emotional consequences be for us if we were to part?
- What would happen to the children if we left each other?
- Are we able to reach a compromise?
- Are we prepared to talk with a relationship counsellor?
- Shall we try a temporary separation which would give us both time to consider what we want and what is possible? How long should such a separation be?

Explore your own feelings

Besides talking to your partner, you also need to explore your own feelings about the relationship.

The following questions might prove helpful. Add any others which come to you.

- Do I still love my partner, in spite of everything that has happened?
- Do I want to spend the rest of my life with my partner?
- What will I do if I leave?
- What effect will ending my relationship have on the children, and how do I balance that against my needs?
- Is my relationship preventing me from doing anything I believe to be essential to my existence?
- I do not want my partner to leave, but what will happen if he or she stays unwillingly?
- How do I handle guilt?
- What is important to me in a relationship, and what compromises, if any, am I prepared to make?

Too much talking

While talking with your partner about your relationship and what has gone wrong is often beneficial, there is a danger of becoming obsessive and talking about little else. This is particularly so if your partner has had an affair and you want to know more details than he or she is prepared to give and which might not be helpful for you to know.

If you wish to save the relationship, try to recharge its batteries by finding activities which you can enjoy together. This will help to give you both a well-needed break from interminable discussions which can become fruitless, exhausting and even defeating of your aim.

Timing of discussions

Without being too bureaucratic about the timing of your discussions, it can be a good idea to try to allocate a specific time for talking, even if you are unable to keep to it. This approach can help you to think about the issues you want to discuss and make your discussions more productive.

Remember, however, that you are after all human, and sometimes the most rewarding discussions take place when they are totally unplanned.

Relationship counselling

After your preliminary discussions, you may both agree that it would be better to explore your relationship problems in a safe environment, with a counsellor. Counselling is not only about saving relationships, it can also help you to reach the conclusion that your relationship has no future and to deal with the practical consequences of your decision.

Choose your counsellor carefully. If you can find one by personal recommendation, so much the better. Any good counsellor will meet with you before you commit yourselves to relationship counselling. It is important that you all feel able to work with each other; there is little point in seeing a counsellor to whom you, or your partner, cannot relate.

A relationship counsellor is there for both partners and will not take sides. Some couples enter counselling in the belief that the counsellor will solve their problems for them. They would like the counsellor to tell them what to do, and how to get the other partner to change his or her behaviour, or personality, to save the relationship.

No good counsellor will even attempt this impossible task. What counselling can do is to encourage you to question and discuss, and help you to understand, your own behaviour and the part you play in your relationship. This knowledge can result in a change in your or your partner's conduct, or allow you to accept what may be unchange-able. It is a process which helps you to find your own way forward and deal with whatever difficulties are confronting you, which, of course, can mean deciding to leave each other.

Information about counselling resources can be found in 'Useful addresses'.

My partner won't talk

Some partners find it very difficult to talk and may resist all efforts to discuss what has gone wrong. They may, of course, have already decided that they are going to leave and that there is little point in talking about anything other than practical arrangements.

If you are in this situation, do consider talking to a counsellor on your own. It will give you the opportunity to explore your own role in the relationship, which will help you to understand yourself better and will certainly prove to be helpful in any new relationship.

Counselling can also be enormously supportive if you do not want your relationship to end and are finding it hard to accept that it is over. It should be not just a handholding exercise, more a process which will help you to grow in your understanding of yourself and move forward.

Talking with friends and family

Although friends and family can be supportive, do be wary of what you decide to tell them, and in how much detail. The advice they offer will usually reflect their view of relationships, and in particular their own, rather than an objective view of your situation. They may fear having to confront their feelings about their own less than perfect relationships if you and your partner break up.

Like many people, your friends and family may find living with uncertainty difficult, and may try to persuade you to make an immediate decision one way or the other about your future. It will make them feel happier.

A further problem is that relationship breakdown destroys social circles because friends and family often find it necessary to side with one partner or the other. To remain friends with both partners when they are at war with each other requires enormous sensitivity and an ability to keep the confidences of both partners. Few people are able to do this and they would rather you stayed together for the benefit of their social world.

Even if you decide to talk to your friends and family, beware of telling them too much. If you become reconciled with your partner, they may not be happy about accepting him or her back into the fold. They may feel unable to forgive your partner for what he or she did. They may also feel embarrassed that they know too much about your private life.

Remind yourself repeatedly that this is your relationship and only you can decide what you want or what is possible for you.

Reconciliation

If you and your partner do decide that you want to remain together, try to be honest about your motives for doing so. Many couples take a pragmatic approach and decide to stay together because they are worried about children, property, finances, employment, religious or cultural beliefs, family pressure or fear of being alone, rather than a desire to be reconciled in a loving, functioning, emotional relationship.

Do not necessarily reject this approach; relationships based on practical concerns can work if you both have similar motives for staying together, and may eventually lead to you and your partner loving and caring for each other. If you do not share the same motives, your relationship is likely to fail. You will all be familiar with the political or other public figure whose relationship goes through difficulties. The press conference is held and undying love and commitment sworn by the couple. Some months later the relationship ends because one partner was trying to save his or her career and the other partner was trying to salvage the relationship for emotional reasons.

If you and your partner decide to stay together, ongoing relationship counselling can be helpful if you are both committed to it.

Temporary separation

If your relationship has become very fraught or you are dithering about whether to leave or stay, it may be helpful for you to separate temporarily. This will give you and your partner time to consider whether you want to spend your future together or remain permanently apart. It will also help you to think about the practical consequences of any decision you might make.

Before beginning the separation, try to agree a time limit. Six months is a reasonable period to give yourselves to reach a decision. If you do not agree a limit, it is all too easy to find yourselves in limbo, living apart but not able to move on with your lives. Accept that you may not keep rigidly to the time limit but aim to keep as close to it as possible. You will need to discuss financial arrangements and childcare, if appropriate, for the period you will be apart. You will find more information on temporary separation in Chapter 2.

2

The end has come: what now?

The interim period – a change of focus

If you decide that your relationship cannot be rescued and that the legal end is inevitable, you will move into a new phase. The nature of your dealings with your partner will now change, and your focus will centre more on practical matters and, in particular, the legal process of ending the relationship and the redistribution of your property and other assets. It requires courage to make practical decisions when you may still feel emotionally very wobbly. Remember that broken hearts, feelings of guilt and other highly charged emotions do not disappear overnight.

However, you cannot remain in limbo for ever. If you do not make plans for your future, your partner may. It is always better to be involved in the planning process than to have someone else's solution forced upon you.

This interim period can feel very unpredictable until your plans begin to take shape, but by dealing with the practicalities which confront you now, you will find the chaos will begin to subside and you will move forward to a more stable place.

Don't be tempted to put off planning your future because you secretly hope that your partner might come back to you. Although miracles do occasionally happen, it is better at this stage to forget such a possibility. In the rare event that your partner does return, you can always revise your plans and begin a new life together.

Planning your future

Where to begin

There are a number of important issues to think about and actions to take in this interim period, and the extent of the task confronting you can feel very overwhelming. It will be much easier for you if you break it up into smaller manageable stages and deal with each one in turn.

You will have appointments to keep and deadlines to meet, so a large desk diary or an electronic diary is an absolute essential. Make sure that it has plenty of space for notes and lists of what to do as well as contact details. Not only will you have all the information in one place, you will also be able to monitor your progress, which will give you a sense of achievement.

A file with an indexing system will help you keep all your legal and other important documents in one place. It is crucial, if you are moving out of the family home into temporary accommodation, that you take copies of all personal and financial information with you.

When your emotional life is shaky, you may feel better if you can keep the practical aspects of your life in order. However, don't ignore your emotional needs. Many people find keeping an emotional diary alongside a practical one can help. Unloading what is in your head on to paper can reduce stress, and you will be able to review your emotional progress as you look back over time at your earlier entries.

Questions to ponder

The following questions should help you in your planning process. You will probably want to add more of your own.

- How will you survive financially?
- What property and financial assets do you or your partner own?
- Who will live in the family home?
- How can you protect your rights in the family home?
- What arrangements do you want to make for your children?
- Who needs to be informed that you and your partner are splitting up?
- Do you want to engage a lawyer or would you prefer to take care of the legal process yourself?

You will also want to think about the legal options open to you to end your relationship. There is detailed information about these in Chapters 3 and 4.

Do not jump the gun at this stage and try to organize the rest of your life. Once the legalities have been finalized, your life will almost certainly change again. Remind yourself that this is an interim stage which usually requires short-term solutions.

Financial survival

Financial matters and children tend to be the most hotly disputed issues when couples split up, and for the majority of people this interim period will be financially complicated. You will need to organize your financial affairs and budget on a temporary basis, while at the same time planning your long-term financial future.

Your assets

This is the time to gather as much information as possible about your own income and other assets as well as those of your partner. It is not always easy to find out about your partner's situation and you may have to do some serious detective work.

Be realistic

Rather surprisingly, many partners find it difficult to accept that if there are insufficient financial resources, they will have no choice but to compromise and accept a lower standard of living or earn more money. A childish mentality can take over at a time of stress, and there can be expectations that, somehow or other, resources should be available even if it is obvious that they are not. This type of approach merely delays the legal end of a relationship and increases the costs.

Budget

Agree a realistic interim budget with your partner. Remember to include all items on which you spend money both regularly and irregularly. It is easier to forget the latter. Although your present budget must be based on the financial resources currently available, it can be used as a starting point in negotiations with your partner about your financial future.

A good computer programme makes drawing up a budget easy, but even a simple spreadsheet can work satisfactorily.

If you are unable to agree a budget with your partner or there are insufficient resources to meet your basic needs, there are a number of things which you can do to help yourself.

Apply to the court for interim maintenance

Partners have a legal duty to support each other until the relationship has legally ended. If your partner fails to maintain you and he or she has sufficient resources to do so, and you do not have the means to support yourself, you may apply to court for an interim maintenance order.

State benefits

If neither of you have sufficient resources to maintain yourselves, you may be able to claim state benefits (see 'Useful addresses' for details of where to obtain advice).

Loans

You may be able to negotiate a short-term loan if you know that there will be money available once the legal process is over and all your property and other assets have been redistributed.

Talk to your bank and other financial institutions

It is essential that you talk to your bank, credit card providers and any other financial institutions as soon as possible. If you and your partner have joint accounts, you may need to freeze the accounts.

Find out your responsibility for any existing debts. If possible, set up accounts and credit cards in your own name.

You must also make sure that your partner cannot run up further debts in the future without your agreement or knowledge. Relationship breakdown is expensive and debts can rapidly increase at this time without either partner realizing it, or because one of you is deliberately spending in retaliation for the other's behaviour. Remember to change passwords and PINs to prevent your partner continuing to use accounts without your agreement.

Other financially related matters

If you remain in the family home alone, you will need to transfer utility accounts such as water, electricity, gas, oil, telephone and council tax into your name. If you do not, you risk services being suspended if your partner fails to pay them. You may also wish to transfer the TV licence and house contents and building insurance into your own name.

Do take a look at your car insurance. If you have been insured as the named driver on your partner's policy, you will usually find that there is a significant increase in the premium when you take out insurance in your own name. If you are to build up your own insurance record, now might be the time to begin.

If you have had private medical insurance provided by your partner's employer, check whether, and for how long, it will continue. If you want to pay for medical insurance in your own right, check with the provider about cover. You may find that pre-existing medical conditions will not be eligible for treatment.

Find employment

If you did not work before, it may now be necessary for you to do so. This could prove to be a positive move in that it will take you out of the home and force you into thinking about matters other than the end of your relationship. The social contact which most work provides can be invaluable; remaining isolated at this time is not generally a good idea.

If you have not worked for a long time, you may need to refresh your qualifications or retrain for a new type of work. Check out all possibilities and think creatively. What are you good at? What do you like doing? Let friends and acquaintances know that you are looking for work. Register with employment agencies and read the employment pages of the newspapers or on the internet. Prepare, or get professional help in preparing, an up-to-date CV to send to prospective employers.

If you have children, you may have to find part-time work or arrange childcare. Make sure that all your earnings will not be eaten up with the costs of childcare.

Educate yourself about financial matters

If you have not taken responsibility for financial matters to date, now is the time to do so. Educate yourself; the weekend newspapers and the internet (if used carefully) can be good sources of information.

Financial retribution

Some partners have been known to go on a spending spree or destroy property as a form of revenge. One woman delivered her husband's fine wine collection to the inhabitants of the village in which they lived when she learned of his affair. Other partners have destroyed well-loved shoe collections, or cut off the arms and legs of expensive suits.

While it is understandable that venting your emotional distress and anger might make you feel temporarily better, it is not advisable to do so. It will anger your partner and may rebound on you in future financial negotiations because you have wasted resources. Try to use your energies to a more positive end.

Financial effect of new relationships

If you are contemplating a new relationship, you need to be aware that it might have a financial effect on any interim maintenance payments or state benefits which you may be receiving. These could be reduced or taken away completely if you begin to share a new home with a cohabitant (see Chapter 5).

Wills

If you and your partner have made wills in each other's favour, you may wish to alter them now. If you fail to alter your will, you and your partner will inherit from each other if either of you were to die in this interim period.

If you have not made a will, do so now. Under English law, if you die without a will your partner will automatically inherit the first £250,000 of your estate if you have children, and the first £450,000 if you do not.

Remember that you will also need to make a new will after the legal end of your relationship.

Where to live

One of the most difficult decisions to make in this interim period is where each partner will live, and it can require great sensitivity to resolve this issue. For most couples, the family home will have been a safe haven. Giving it up can be emotionally destabilizing and may cause huge resentment. If you are the partner leaving, you may need considerable support to cope with the feeling of dislocation until you are able to establish a permanent home for yourself once more.

Live separately

In spite of the problems for the partner who moves out of the home, it is normally preferable to live separately at this time. Few couples can remain amicably in the family home while in the death throes of their relationship.

Who should move out?

Stability for children

If you have children, it will usually be better for the parent with whom they are to live to remain in the family home. It will give the children the stability they need. If you are the parent who has to move out, try to make sure that you are able to accommodate your children in your new home for overnight visits. There is nothing more difficult than trying to keep a relationship with your children intact if you have no satisfactory place for them to stay with you.

Practical considerations

If there are no children to take into account, you and your partner will have to try to reach agreement over who should move out. Often the decision will be made on practical grounds, such as proximity to work or the availability of financial resources to buy or rent alternative accommodation.

A temporary solution

Remember that any arrangement reached at this stage is often temporary. The partner who remains in the home may lose sight of this and expect that he or she will remain there after the legal formalities are over. In many cases, it will then be necessary for the family home to be sold or, if rented, exchanged for less expensive accommodation.

Remaining in the family home together

In difficult economic times, you may have to remain in the family home together. It may not be easy to sell the property, or there may be insufficient resources to pay for alternative accommodation.

You may, of course, choose to live in the family home together to give your children time to adjust to the new situation, or because you must continue to share the care of a sick or disabled child, or because your family home is tied accommodation. If your partner is elderly, ill or disabled, you may also feel obliged to stay until other arrangements can be made.

It will be preferable if you can divide the property in some way, albeit on a temporary basis, so that you each have your own space. If you are to share in an amicable manner, you will also need to discuss some ground rules relating to childcare, everyday expenditure on food and utilities, and visitors, particularly if either of you has started a new relationship. (See Chapter 3 for the effect of living together and the options for legally ending your relationship.)

You should also discuss how long the sharing arrangement should last. If you know that this potentially difficult situation will only be for a limited time, it should be easier for you to cope with it. Of course, if you are dependent on selling the property, the matter will not be under your control.

Protecting your home

Ownership of the family home is legally complex. If you are unsure about any of the rights discussed below, you must talk to a lawyer to make sure that you protect yourself as far as possible from losing your home or your share in it.

What rights do you have?

Joint ownership

Where the family home is owned by both of you, neither of you will be able to use it as security for new loans, or sell it, without the agreement of both of you. Similarly, if you rent your home and both your names are on the lease, neither of you will be able to sub-let or terminate the lease without each other's agreement.

If you are joint owners of the family home, you must check whether you are joint tenants; many couples are. This means that if the property is sold you will share the proceeds equally. If either of you were to die, the family home would be owned outright by the surviving partner. There would be no share left for anyone else to inherit. If you do not want this to happen, you will need to consult a lawyer and ask for the joint tenancy to be severed and changed into a tenancy in common. This would allow you to separate your share from your partner's and leave it in your will to anyone you wish.

Property in the name of one partner

If the family home is in the name of your partner, you should consult a lawyer to find out whether you have acquired any rights in it. It is possible that you may have done so if your partner informally agreed that you could have a share, and you contributed financially to its purchase or improvement, or made practical improvements yourself. Your lawyer will advise you on how to protect such a right and prevent your partner from using the family home as security for loans, or selling it.

A right to occupy the family home

If you do not own your home jointly with your partner and have not acquired any other right in it, you have a right to occupy it until the legal end of your relationship. You do need to register your right with the Land Registry (see 'Useful addresses' for further details) to protect you if your partner tries to sell the family home or borrow against it. Any buyer or lender would then know about your right of occupation and would be bound by it in the same way as your partner. You will not be protected against any purchaser or lender who entered into a deal with your partner before you registered your right.

Mortgages, secured loans and rent

It is essential that any mortgage or secured loan against the family home, or rent, continues to be paid, otherwise you risk losing it and becoming homeless. If there is any doubt in your mind that payments cannot be, or are not being, paid, you must talk to your mortgage provider, bank or other financial institution or landlord. Explain the situation and discuss what temporary arrangements can be made to deal with the problem.

Remember that in certain circumstances your partner may have a right to make further borrowings against the family home without your knowledge. You should contact any loan provider as soon as possible to check whether this is possible and, if so, whether you can do anything to limit the borrowings.

When times are financially difficult, there may be a temptation for one partner to attempt to borrow against the security of the home. You may be asked to sign financial documents to allow this to happen. If you are asked to do this, make sure that you read any document very carefully to make sure that you fully understand its consequences. If in doubt, do not sign. Seek legal advice; you must be sure that you are not signing your home away.

If you claim state benefits, you may be able to claim the interest payments, up to a maximum level, on any mortgage or loan in your name secured against the family home. If the family home is rented, you may be able to obtain housing benefit from your local authority.

Protecting your children

Cooperate

Do everything possible to cooperate with your partner over the arrangements for your children at this time. You are both still their parents, and it is not their fault that your relationship has gone wrong.

What to tell children

Children are often aware that something worrying is happening but do not know exactly what it is. If possible, you should both talk to them and reassure them that, although you may be going to live apart, you will both continue to love them and continue to play an important part in their lives.

Try to be led by their questions. How much you tell children and what to say obviously depends on their age.

You will find more detailed information on what to tell children in Chapter 6.

Violent relationships – a special note

If you are involved in a violent relationship, you must make efforts to protect yourself and your children before you consider doing anything else.

Do not hesitate to dial 999 if you or your children are in immediate danger. If the danger is not imminent and you can find a way of persuading your partner to leave the family home, do so. This is not an easy thing to do and you may not succeed. Talk with a lawyer or your local police domestic violence unit. All police forces have specially trained staff who will decide what action to take and will advise you on how to apply for court orders to protect you from further harm. In certain circumstances, the court can exclude your partner from the family home and the area around it. You may be provided with a mobile phone to contact the police at any time. It may be necessary for you to change the locks on your home.

You may have to leave your home and stay with family or friends on a temporary basis. If these options are not open to you, you should contact your local Social Services department or a domestic violence organization to help find you short-term housing (for more information see 'Useful addresses').

Whom to tell

Because this is a time of uncertainty about the future, there is a temptation not to inform too many people about your situation. You may be too distressed or embarrassed to do so, or you may feel that you would rather wait until the legal process is finally over. There are, however, some people and institutions who do need to know now.

If you have not already told your family and friends because you find it too difficult and are afraid of their reaction, consider writing to them. Explain briefly that you and your partner are splitting up. You do not need to go into detail about what has happened unless you wish to. Let them know what support you would like them to give, or whether you would simply like to keep in touch with them. Don't forget to give them any new contact details.

The following list will provide a guide to institutions you may need to tell and provide with any new contact details:

- mortgage lender
- landlord
- housing benefit office
- social security office
- tax office
- your children's present school and future school if they are about to move to a new one
- bank and credit card companies
- the Post Office for redirection of your mail
- doctor, dentist and any other health providers
- insurance companies
- executors of your will.

Engaging a lawyer or going it alone

If you and your partner are able to cooperate over the arrangements for your children and the redistribution of your property and other assets (provided that these are not substantial or complex), it is perfectly possible for you to manage the entire legal process yourself. The relevant forms are readily available on the internet, and there are a number of resources available to help you complete them (see 'Useful addresses' for details).

The advantage of acting for yourself is that you will be able to keep the whole process, including costs, under your control. You might also find psychological benefits in going it alone; there can be a very real sense of achievement in mastering the legal process.

If you are at war with your partner over property, finances or children, or if your property and financial affairs are complex, you will have to seek the advice of an experienced family lawyer.

Even if your affairs are simple, you may be daunted by the complexities of the law and the legal process and would feel more comfortable handing everything over to a lawyer.

Legal fees

The costs of using a lawyer are not insignificant. In simple cases where you and your partner are not in dispute, a lawyer might agree to a fixed fee to complete the legal process for you. If so, it is unlikely to be less than £500 plus the cost of court fees, letters, emails and telephone calls (known as disbursements) if you are the partner who begins the legal process (the petitioner). The fee for your partner (the respondent) is unlikely to be less than £400 plus disbursements. There would be further fees for dealing with agreements for the division of your assets and the arrangements for your children.

The more complex your affairs, the higher will be your legal fees because your lawyer will charge by the hour. The hourly fee will depend on your lawyer's experience and office location. You can expect to pay anywhere between £200 and £800 per hour.

You should always discuss legal fees with your lawyer before he or she begins to work for you. Everything should be put in writing for you so that you understand exactly what the terms of your agreement are.

Remember that visits to lawyers are not social calls and lawyers are not emotional counsellors, no matter how sympathetic they may try to be. They are in business. Try to avoid indulging in long weeping sessions in your lawyer's office; they will be expensive tears.

Long-drawn-out battles with your partner using your lawyer as an intermediary will also be expensive and there will be fewer assets available at the end of the day. Do not do as one angry farmer did: he telephoned his divorce lawyer on a daily basis to report his wife's latest extravagances. On one occasion, he asked his lawyer to intervene because she was disposing of the old jam jars he had squirrelled away in the interests of household economy. One dreads to think of the final bill he was forced to pay.

A non-confrontational way forward

It is generally accepted that confrontation should be avoided if at all possible when going through the legal process. There are a number of ways which might help you and your partner to cooperate rather than wage war with each other (see 'Useful addresses' for further details).

Mediation

Mediation is a process which aims to help partners reach agreement about their property and financial affairs, and arrangements for their children, without going to court and letting the judge decide for them.

If you opt for mediation, you choose an independent trained mediator who will meet with you and your partner in an attempt to find a solution satisfactory to you both. Mediators cannot take sides with either of you. If they are also lawyers, they may not give you legal advice but may only explain to you what the law is; the dividing line is a fine one.

Choosing a mediator Before you decide on mediation, you need to meet with the proposed mediator to make sure that you feel able to work with him or her, and find out what you can expect to happen during the process and how much it will cost. There is no standard fee. If you have little capital or are on a low income or receiving state benefits, you may be eligible to have your mediation paid for with funding from the Community Legal Service (CLS) (<www.legalservices.gov.uk>). In general, you can expect mediation to take about six hours in total.

Advantages of mediation Mediation has the advantage of avoiding the to-ing and fro-ing of legal letters and, in theory, should be non-confrontational and less expensive and shorter than any other legal process. You will, hopefully, learn how to cooperate with your partner, something that will be particularly beneficial if you have children.

A confidential process Whatever you say during the mediation sessions is strictly confidential. The only exception is if something arises which would be a threat to the life of either partner or the welfare of your children, when your mediator would be forced to take action.

If you are unable to reach agreement with your partner and have to let the court decide for you, you may reveal to the court the property and financial information which was given to you during the mediation sessions. You may not, however, reveal the content of any tentative discussions which you and your partner had about how you might divide the assets between you.

Compromise If you choose to use mediation, be prepared to compromise; it is impossible for you both to get your own way. If you succeed in reaching an agreement, it will be recorded in writing by your mediator. You may then take it to a lawyer for it to be drawn up into a formal legal document, or you may choose to do that yourself; this document can then be confirmed by the court as a legally enforceable consent order after your relationship has been legally ended (see Chapter 5).

Disadvantages of mediation The mediation process is not appropriate for everyone. A fragile person, particularly one who has experienced domestic violence, may be afraid of meeting a tough partner face to face, and may also feel under pressure to reach an agreement.

A further disadvantage is that you will have to pay the mediator for the mediation process, as well as a lawyer, if you are using one, to draw up the agreement. If the process fails you will still have to pay the mediation fees and the costs of going to court.

Collaborative law

Rather than spend time with a mediator, you and your partner may prefer to each choose a lawyer who practises collaborative law. Once you have chosen your lawyers, you will all get together in a number of four-way meetings to negotiate an agreement without going to court.

Advantages of collaborative law   The advantage of using the collaborative law process is that your lawyer will be by your side throughout all the negotiations, to ensure that you understand what is happening and that the outcome is a fair one for you. There will be no necessity for legal letters to wing back and forth, and the process will be a very open one. The timing of meetings and the time period for concluding negotiations is entirely dependent on you and your partner. You will not be bound by the dates of court hearings which are never under your control.

Once you have reached an agreement, it can be confirmed by the court as a legally enforceable consent order.

Disadvantages of collaborative law   There are disadvantages to collaborative law. First, you will each have the expense of employing your own lawyer. Second, one of the rules of collaborative law is that if the process fails and you are unable to reach an agreement, your lawyers will not be able to continue to work for you. You will each have to find a new lawyer, or go it alone, to reach an agreement, or let the court decide for you.

Resolution

Resolution is the name of an association of family lawyers who are committed to a non-confrontational approach. Its members are required to deal with each other in a civilized way, and to encourage their clients to reach fair agreements. You may wish to make sure that you use a lawyer who belongs to Resolution.

Take care of yourself

It is essential that you take good care of yourself during this interim period. Even if you are the one who wants to leave the relationship, it can be lonely and stressful with or without a potential new partner, particularly if you have left behind the security of your home and children. Try to make sure that you have an adequate support system on which you can rely.

Support systems

Professional help

You need to be aware that emotional stress can have a very bad effect on your physical and mental health. It may require the same approach to recovery as in the case of physical illness.

If you are depressed or stressed, do not be embarrassed to talk frankly to your doctor, who should be able to help you decide whether you need short-term medication, counselling or some other form of therapy.

Good friends

Find out who are the close friends on whom you can call for support when times feel very rough. You may even discover new supportive friends at this time who have had similar experiences to yours.

Whether your friends are new or old, don't overwhelm them. Even very good friends have limits when bombarded daily with one-sided conversations of the latest developments in your relationship break-down. Agree with them about the sort of dire practical or emotional emergency which makes it permissible for you to call them in the middle of the night. Support can also be gained from spending time with friends without discussing your problems.

If possible, spend time with friends who are not prejudiced about your partner and who are capable of giving you sensible and com-paratively unbiased advice. This may be a counsel of perfection if your partner has behaved very badly. Your friends will be more concerned about protecting you from further damage than being unbiased.

Accept offers of help without worrying about whether you can recip-rocate at this point. There will be plenty of time in the future when your friends will need your support.

Remember that one of the fallouts from the breakdown of your relationship is the loss of friends whom you shared with your partner. As we saw in Chapter 1, some friends will side with one partner rather than the other. They may also be unable to deal with your vulnerability, or may fear that you will become a predator on their partners.

Indulge yourself

This is a time when you need to be a little self-indulgent and treat yourself in whatever way makes you feel better.

Although you may not feel like going away, if you can afford a short break with a supportive friend it can be helpful to escape for a little while. And yes, you will still have to face the situation when you return, but you may feel slightly stronger to do so.

Try to avoid going to destinations you went to with your partner. They are likely to remind you of the happy – or even unhappy – times which you spent together, and that is unlikely to be helpful at this time.

Eat and sleep

Do ensure that you feed yourself properly. Losing weight may appear to be one of the good side effects of emotional stress but it will not necessarily do much for your health; nor will overeating to console yourself. Think of all that dieting you will have to do once you recover.

It is often not easy to sleep at times of stress, and getting overtired can increase the stress. Temporary medication, acupuncture, massage or relaxation tapes can all help. If you have small children who also keep you awake, ask family or friends to take care of them from time to time to allow you to sleep. It is surprising how much better life seems when one is not sleep-deprived.

Take care of your appearance

Don't neglect how you look. Rebuilding self-confidence is important, particularly if you are the one who has been abandoned.

Check out your wardrobe and try to indulge in some judicious purchases if you are able to afford them. If you are in depressed mode, take a good friend with you to ensure that you do not buy depressing clothes.

Exercise, apart from having a good effect on your figure, can also lift your spirits, and they will probably need plenty of boosting. If you are not a lover of gyms or health clubs, take a walk on a regular basis.

Give yourself time

Take your time in making practical decisions about your future. Do not be pushed into following anyone else's time-scale. However, do not delay excessively; set yourself some limits. Making decisions can help the healing process.

If you are leaving your partner for a new relationship, take time to decide about its future. The relationship may have been the catalyst which triggered your departure but it may not be a lasting one.

Do not despair

Remind yourself continually that no matter how difficult life feels now, it will get better. Believe in yourself and your ability to recover. There is a worthwhile life ahead of you with or without a new partner.

3

Ending the relationship: your legal options

The options open to you

Once you have decided to bring your relationship to a legal end, you have the option of applying for a decree of divorce or judicial separation if you are married, or a dissolution order or separation order if you are a civil partner. In a limited number of circumstances a spouse may be able to apply for a decree of nullity and a civil partner a nullity order; these will be explained in Chapter 4.

Although same-sex partners were given the same rights as married couples by the Civil Partnership Act 2004 (which came into effect in 2005), the government was not prepared to risk a backlash from the electorate by allowing them to marry. As a consequence, it was forced to use different language in the Act for the legal processes which begin and end civil partnerships. In spite of this, you will find that there is a common tendency in the media and in popular speech to use the same language for these legal processes.

As yet, few dissolution orders or separation orders have been granted. Between 2005 and 2008, there were only 108 dissolution orders and three separation orders. One of the first dissolution orders took place in January 2009 between Matt Lucas, a comedian, and a television producer, Kevin McGee.

In this chapter the legal options and their requirements for both married couples and civil partners to end their relationships are considered alongside each other because they are remarkably similar. Inevitably, the majority of the examples given refer to married couples because of the lack of cases involving civil partners. Regardless of whether you are a spouse or a civil partner, and regardless of the option you choose, the partner who makes the application for a decree or order (known as the petition) is called the petitioner, and the other partner is called the respondent.

Decrees of divorce and dissolution orders

The majority of partners are likely to opt for a decree of divorce or a dissolution order, because once you have obtained your decree or order you lose the status of spouse or civil partner and are free to marry again or enter into a new civil partnership. If you and your partner change your minds after the decree or order has been granted, you will have to remarry or enter into a new civil partnership to regain your status. The actors Elizabeth Taylor and Richard Burton regretted their divorce and remarried each other 16 months later. Their remarriage only lasted nine months.

The decree or order allows you to agree, or the court to decide, how your property and other assets should be divided, and the arrangements for your children (see Chapters 5 and 6).

Decrees of judicial separation and separation orders

Decrees of judicial separation and separation orders also allow you to make legal arrangements about your property and other assets, and your children's future, or let the court decide them for you. They do not, however, allow you or your partner to remarry or enter into a new civil partnership. It is comparatively unusual for couples to take the separation route.

Separation is an end in itself, and not a stage en route to a decree of divorce or a dissolution order, although some couples who have separated may decide subsequently to divorce or obtain a dissolution order.

For the purposes of this book, separation will be treated as ending the relationship, because in reality that is what it does. Although technically you remain a spouse or civil partner, you will see that this has few practical consequences for you.

The requirements

To the surprise of many partners, you cannot end your relationship on demand. The state encourages marriage and civil partnership because it sees them as important for the stability of society. When you marry or become a civil partner, whether you realize it or not you agree to let the state involve itself in your relationship. The legal obligation of financially supporting your partner (and the moral obligation of caring for him or her) is given to you. This takes pressure off the state, and in return it gives you certain legal advantages which are not available to those who have chosen only to cohabit.

Because the state is involved in your relationship, you must meet certain legal requirements if you want to end it. You will then be given the benefit of further legal advantages to help you deal with your property and other assets, and make arrangements for your children's future. The requirements are unlikely to present any major obstacle for you, other than the expenditure of a rather large amount of emotional energy and, if you decide to engage a lawyer, money.

A valid marriage or valid civil partnership

It may seem rather obvious that the most important of all the require-ments is that you must have been validly married or entered into a valid civil partnership (see Chapters 2 and 3 of Welstead and Edwards for information on the validity of relationships; details in 'Further reading'). Somewhat surprisingly, there are couples who believe them-selves to be in a valid legal relationship and only realize that they are not when they try to end it. They will probably be entitled to a decree or order of nullity (see Chapter 4).

If you are a same-sex couple who married in a country where same-sex marriage is permitted and you come to live in the UK, your relationship will automatically be treated as a valid civil partnership. Two British university professors, Sue Wilkinson and Celia Kitzinger, married in Canada in 2003, while one of them was working there. On their return to England, they protested that their relationship had been downgraded because they were treated as civil partners and not spouses. They tried to get their marriage legally recognized here but were unsuccessful.

The one-year rule

The law does not allow you to petition for divorce or a dissolution order until you have been married or in a civil partnership for one year. The reason for this is to encourage couples to take marriage and civil partnerships seriously and not to give up on their relationship too soon. This rule can be harsh if you are living in a very difficult relationship without any hope of improvement or reconciliation. Even if you discover your partner to be violent, or a liar, or a cheat, or of a different sexual orientation from what you had thought, you must still wait for one year to go by. This does not, of course, mean that you must continue to live together. You may very well decide that it would be better to live apart until the year is over. If you are in a violent relationship, it is essential that you do so to protect yourself.

Once you have been married or in a civil partnership for one year, you may base your petition for divorce or a dissolution order on events that occurred during that first year.

The one-year rule does not apply to decrees of judicial separation or separation orders. You may apply for these at any time.

Domiciled or habitually resident in the jurisdiction of England and Wales

For the majority of couples, the issue of domicile and habitual residence will be irrelevant. Both you and your partner are likely to meet the requirements of domicile and habitual residence because you have always lived in the jurisdiction.

However, some partners may be in an international relationship. For instance, you and your partner may be from different countries, have married or entered into a civil partnership in a third country, and live in a fourth country. You may want to start legal proceedings here partly because you believe (and usually quite rightly) that there are financial advantages to be gained from doing so. If you are involved in an international relationship, the rules relating to domicile and habitual residence are quite complex and you should consult a lawyer who specializes in international family law. In brief, to have the right to begin proceedings in England and Wales,

- both spouses or civil partners must be habitually resident or domiciled here; or
- both spouses or civil partners were jointly resident or domiciled here and one of them is still habitually resident here; or
- the petitioner or applicant has been habitually resident here for the last 12 months; or
- the respondent is habitually resident here; or
- the petitioner or applicant is domiciled and habitually resident here and has resided here for at least the last six months.

Irretrievable breakdown of your relationship

There is only one ground for a decree of divorce or a dissolution order and that is your relationship must have irretrievably broken down. It is not sufficient merely to state that this is so. If you are a spouse, you must prove one of five facts relating to your relationship. If you are a civil partner, you must prove one of four of these five facts. It will be a very rare couple whose relationship has irretrievably broken down who cannot prove one of the relevant facts.

If you are petitioning for a decree of judicial separation or a separation order, you simply have to prove one of the five facts if you are a spouse, and one of four of the five facts if you are a civil partner. Irretrievable breakdown is irrelevant.

The five facts

Fact 1: Adultery and intolerability

This first fact is fault-based; it requires you to make an accusation against your partner. It is the only fact which cannot be used by civil partners. The government wished to avoid any embarrassment of trying to define what adultery might mean in the context of a same-sex relationships, and simply decided that same-sex partners are biologically incapable of adultery with a person of the same sex. It failed to consider the possibility that a civil partner might have a heterosexual relationship during a civil partnership. However, you will probably be able to rely on fact 2 (behaviour which you cannot reasonably be expected to live with, see p. 31), if your partner has any sexual relationship outside your civil partnership.

A significant number of those who petition for divorce or judicial separation rely on this fact, and they are more likely to be women. Even in these days of equality, men are much more likely to commit adultery than women.

Definition of adultery   To petition for divorce using this fact, your spouse must have had voluntary penetrative sexual intercourse with a member of the opposite sex. Sex which falls short of this is not adultery. President Clinton's famous statement that he had not committed adultery with Monica Lewinsky was strictly speaking correct even though he admitted to having engaged in oral sex.

> A couple who met in an internet chat room married and reinvented themselves in the virtual world known as Second Life. The husband began an adulterous virtual relationship with the virtual persona created

by a woman online in America. His wife protested and petitioned for divorce. Because virtual adultery is not adultery for the purposes of divorce, she was forced to rely on fact 2. The husband went to live with the American woman.

Voluntary act   The sex must have been a voluntary act. A woman who has been raped has not committed adultery because she did not consent.

Polygamy   Although you may not marry polygamously in England and Wales, the law recognizes that you may have married legally in a country where polygamy is permitted. If your spouse is having a sexual relationship with you as well as his other wife or wives, this does not count as adultery.

It will be quite unusual for a polygamously married man to have more than one wife here because he can only obtain a spousal visa for one wife. However, his other wives may have entered the country on non-spousal visas. It is believed that there are currently 1,000 valid polygamous marriages in England and Wales.

Same-sex sexual conduct   Where your spouse has engaged in homo-sexual or lesbian sexual behaviour, you may not petition for divorce using the adultery fact; adultery is defined very narrowly as an act between heterosexuals. However, you would be able to rely on fact 2.

Evidence   Gone are the days of those famous scenes from classic films where a private detective follows the maid up to the hotel bedroom to photograph the adulterous couple *in flagrante*. Your statement that your spouse has committed adultery, provided no one denies it, will be sufficient. In spite of this, some spouses prefer to extract a confession from the adulterer. Others employ a detective to produce convincing evidence that adultery has taken place.

If your spouse does deny adultery, you will have to produce evidence. Your wife's conception of a child at a time when you were absent, or DNA evidence which proves that a child cannot be your biological child, will always be sufficient proof of adultery. DNA evidence which strongly suggests that your spouse might be the father of another woman's child may also be evidence of adultery. Statistical evidence suggests that at least 10 per cent of children are not the biological children of the men who believe themselves to be their fathers.

Identity It does not matter whether you know the identity of the person with whom your spouse has committed adultery (the co-respondent). If you do know who it is, you may name him or her in your divorce petition if you wish, but it is not necessary to do so.

Whose adultery? You may not rely on your own adultery in any petition for divorce. However, if your spouse has also committed adultery, your own adultery does not prevent you from petitioning for divorce on the basis of your spouse's adultery.

Intolerability Once you decide to petition using this fact, rather strangely you must also state that you find it intolerable to continue to live with your spouse for some reason other than the adultery. Your reasons for finding it intolerable can be totally trivial. One wife claimed that her husband, who had committed adultery on only one occasion, blew his nose too frequently and that she found it to be intolerable. She was granted a divorce.

The six-month rule You may continue to live with your spouse for up to six months after the adultery took place without losing your right to rely on it in future divorce proceedings. This allows you to attempt to save your marriage. If you continue to live with your spouse for longer than six months, it will be assumed that you do not find it intolerable to live with an adulterous spouse. If you still wish to divorce, you will have to use one of the other five facts, unless, of course, your spouse commits further acts of adultery.

Fact 2: Behaviour which you cannot reasonably be expected to live with

This fault-based fact is the most commonly used of all the five facts. It will be a very rare couple who cannot find some conduct which falls within this category; very few people can live in an intimate relationship without experiencing some aspect of their partner's behaviour as intolerable.

Not unreasonable behaviour Although this fact is commonly referred to as 'unreasonable behaviour', it is not necessary to prove that your partner's behaviour is unreasonable; you simply have to show that you cannot reasonably be expected to live with it. Whether you can or cannot has to be judged by the standards of any normal person, taking into account your particular fragilities and other personal qualities. So, for instance, if your partner is untidy and disorganized, that in itself may not be particularly unreasonable behaviour given his or her personality. If you, however, are a perfectionist, it might be unreasonable to expect you to live with this messy behaviour. Of course, the position could be reversed and your untidy partner could maintain that it is unreasonable to be expected to live with your perfectionist behaviour.

Relevant behaviour The types of behaviour complained about are wide-ranging.

One husband, a very wealthy ship-owner, constantly criticized his wife, and controlled and undermined her to such an extent that she became very depressed. He gave her no regular personal or housekeeping allowance, but made her ask his secretary every time she required money. He refused to have a door key because he wanted to make sure that she remained permanently at home to let him into the house at any time of the day or night. The wife was granted a divorce even though her husband protested that he still loved her and wanted their marriage to continue.

An extreme example of behaviour involved a wife who provided her depressed husband with drugs and alcohol to help him in his attempts to commit suicide. When he failed yet again to kill himself, she told him that he was utterly useless as a husband and that he could not even commit suicide properly. The husband succeeded in obtaining a divorce.

Another husband undertook extensive home renovations, in a totally incompetent manner, for months on end. During that time, he left his wife and teenage daughter living on a building site. He left the lavatory without a door, the floorboards were permanently up, he mixed cement indoors and deposited vast quantities of rubble in the garden which he never cleared away. His wife and daughter were distressed and embarrassed, and found it difficult to invite friends home. The wife was granted a divorce.

It is a little surprising that an emotional reaction to a partner's long-term adultery can be relevant behaviour.

A 75-year-old woman discovered that her husband, who worked away from home during the week, lived with another woman and their 15-year-old child in a house which he had bought for them. His wife did not want to divorce him but she was very angry. She made harassing telephone calls to her husband and his mistress, contacted the local press, and generally spread the news about her husband's behaviour. He applied for a divorce and maintained that his wife's behaviour was such that he could not reasonably be expected to live with it. The divorce was granted.

Passive behaviour   Your partner's behaviour may be passive.

One husband never spoke to his wife, and ignored all bills sent to their home. The bailiffs arrived and confiscated property to satisfy the debts. His wife obtained a divorce because his passive behaviour was such that she could not reasonably be expected to live with it.

Involuntary behaviour   Problems may arise if the behaviour of your partner is caused by an illness or accident. In such circumstances, although the behaviour is without fault, the court is likely to take a sympathetic approach and end your relationship if you are unable to deal with the involuntary behaviour.

Non-behaviour   As yet no court has had to consider whether a partner who has lapsed into a coma can be held to have behaved in a way which it is unreasonable to expect you to live with. It is likely that the same approach would be taken as with involuntary behaviour.

A change of mind   You may have agreed with your partner that a certain type of behaviour is acceptable, but later one of you has a change of mind. For example, if you agreed to use contraception during the marriage and your partner later refuses to do so, this could count as relevant behaviour which would allow you to legally end your relationship.

In theory, your partner could also maintain that your behaviour, in insisting on keeping to the original agreement, is also relevant behaviour.

Fact 3: Two years living apart and agreement to end the relationship

Partners who do not want the public to know the intimate details of their relationship have commonly used this non-fault-based fact. All the royal divorces which have taken place over the last 30 years have relied on this fact. Princess Margaret used it in 1978 when she and Anthony Armstrong-Jones were the first royal couple to divorce since the reign of Henry VIII. Both partners must agree to the petition.

Living apart for two years   You must have been living apart from your partner for two years. You must state in your petition when the two-year period began and the reason for living apart.

Living apart in the same house There may be financial or other practical reasons for having to remain in the same house as your partner for the two-year period. It is possible to continue to live under the same roof and claim to be living apart, but there must be a complete separation of your lives. Living apart like this can be very difficult to achieve where there are children, or where the house is very small or financial resources are limited and food shopping, cooking and meals need to be shared. In difficult economic times, it is possible that a more liberal view will be taken of what it means to live apart.

> One couple claimed to be living apart when the husband, who was ill and could not live alone, moved in with his wife and her cohabitant. The husband paid his wife for taking care of him. The divorce was granted.

Agreement You must also agree to the petition by freely signing a consent form. This means that you will not be able to rely on this fact if you are living apart from a mentally ill or absent partner.

If your partner encouraged you to sign the consent form by giving you misleading information, your agreement will not be valid.

The six-month rule You may begin to live apart from your partner and move back together for up to six months. Any time spent together cannot count towards the two-year requirement. If you remain together for longer than six months, you will have to restart the two-year period of living apart.

Fact 4: Desertion

Desertion, the third fault-based fact, is the least used of all the five facts.

Meaning of desertion To rely on this fact, you must be able to prove that your partner has been absent for two years without your agreement, and does not intend to return.

In most cases this means that your partner will leave the family home. However, it is possible, although almost unheard of, for a partner to remain in the family home and still be in desertion. You must be able to show that he or she has lived a totally separate life from you in every possible way.

No justification for the desertion You must not have behaved in a way which justifies your partner leaving. If you have, you will not be able to claim desertion, and your partner may even be able to claim that you have done the deserting. This is known as constructive or justified desertion. Examples of this type of desertion include leaving your partner because he or she: refuses to have a sexual relationship without a good reason; is violent; has extra-relationship sex; has a mental illness which affects the relationship; or fails to provide essential financial maintenance.

Intention to desert If your partner is working away from home with your agreement, or is in prison, or is absent for other good reasons, this is not desertion because there is no intention to desert. The absence may become desertion if your partner changes his or her mind and decides not to return, and is absent for two years from that date.

If your partner works away from home in spite of your objections, the absence might count as desertion. It will depend on the nature of the work and how reasonable you are being in your objections. It is unlikely that working away as a member of the armed forces, or because there is no other work available close to home, will be regarded as desertion.

Mental incapacity and desertion A partner who is mentally incapable cannot desert. However, if your partner leaves intending to desert and then becomes mentally incapable, he or she may still be in desertion. There must be evidence that your partner's intention to desert would have continued had the mental incapacity not happened. This will be very difficult to prove.

Offers to return If your partner offers to return before the two years have gone by, you must accept the offer unless there are very good reasons not to do so. Such reasons include a fear of violence or a belief that the offer is not a serious one. If you refuse the offer unreasonably, you will become the deserter.

The six-month rule You will not lose your right to rely on your partner's desertion if he or she returns to live with you for up to six months. Any time you spend together will not count towards the two-year requirement.

Fact 5: Five years living apart without agreement

If you are unable to rely on any of the other facts, you may have no choice but to rely on what is regarded as the fact of last resort. It has been referred to as a 'Casanova's charter' for husbands who wish to unilaterally divorce their totally innocent wives. However, the truth is that more women than men have relied on this fact.

You must live apart for five years and there is no requirement for either partner to agree to the petition. It is possible to live apart in the same house providing you lead totally separate lives.

The grave hardship rule It is recognized that the use of this fact can be very hard on a partner, particularly an elderly one who does not want the relationship to end and believes that he or she has done nothing wrong. For this reason the law allows a respondent to object to any decree or order if it will cause serious financial or other hardship and it would in all the circumstances be wrong to grant a divorce or dissolve the civil partnership. The grave hardship rule does not apply to decrees of separation or separation orders. It is very rare for a claim of grave hardship to succeed.

Virtually all partners are likely to suffer some form of hardship because of the breakdown of their relationship. They are likely to be financially less well off and have to move to a new home. However, the grave hardship rule is limited to hardship which results directly from the grant of the decree or order and not merely from the breakdown of the relationship; it is not easy to tell the difference between the two.

Financial hardship Now that pension division is possible (see Chapter 5), it will be difficult for any respondent to prove financial hardship. It may be possible to show that you would lose benefits given to a spouse or civil partner by a partner's employer. Inheritance rights cannot be taken into account because there is no certainty that you would benefit; wills can always be changed up to the moment of death.

You will not be able to claim grave financial hardship if you have sufficient financial resource of your own to compensate for any financial loss.

Other forms of hardship Occasionally respondents have claimed that they would be excluded from their social or religious community if a decree or order were to be granted against their will. None of them have succeeded in preventing the relationship from being legally ended.

Wrong in all the circumstances to grant the decree or order Even if you can show that you would suffer serious hardship, there is one further obstacle to overcome. The court has the final say and will balance out any hardship claimed by you if the decree or order were to be granted, against the hardship which your partner might suffer if the decree or order were to be refused. Courts have shown a reluctance to find that it would be wrong to refuse a decree or order when it is quite clear that there is no possibility of the parties ever becoming reconciled.

The six-month rule   As with all the other facts, you may live together for up to six months and still end your relationship based on the five-year fact. Any time which you spend together during the six-month period will not count towards the five-year period. If you live together for longer than six months, you will have to begin the five-year period again. It will be a brave person who would risk doing this, knowing that if the relationship did not work it would be another five years before a new petition could be brought.

Cooperation or confrontation

More than one of the five facts may apply to your situation and you will have to decide which one to use. There can be a huge temptation, when you feel very angry at your partner's behaviour, to exact vengeance and rely on one of the fault-based facts. There are both advantages and disadvantages to this. The advantages are:

- Acknowledging that your partner is at fault, if that really is the case, may help you to recover more rapidly from what has happened.
- Decrees or orders based on adultery, or the behaviour fact, allow a decree or order to be granted a wait of two or five years.
- Partners who are at fault often feel guilty. They may be more agreeable to negotiate over arrangements for children or agree a more generous division of property and other assets, particularly if they want to begin a new legal relationship.

The disadvantages are:

- Accusations of fault may lead to retaliation by your partner and the use of delaying tactics which will lead to long-drawn-out and unpleasant legal proceedings.
- You may find it more difficult to reach agreement over property and financial matters, and arrangements for children.

Cooperation with your partner may be easier if you choose not to use a fault-based fact when an alternative one is available to you. Remember that fault is not always one-sided; you may have contributed to your partner's conduct or be equally at fault, albeit in a different way.

Don't risk perjury

For most people, the nature of the legal process to end the relationship is such that no serious enquiry will be made about what you say in your petition (see Chapter 7). Don't be tempted, however, to collude with your partner and lie about your relationship. You must remember that if you lie about any fact on which you are relying or about any other matter, and it is discovered, you will not only be denied your decree or order but you will be committing perjury, which is a criminal offence.

Denying your partner's claims

You may be tempted to defend the petition and deny your partner's claims about the relationship, either to make life difficult for him or her or because you genuinely want your relationship to continue. Remember that it is very difficult to prevent a determined partner who believes that the relationship has broken down from obtaining a decree or order. Why waste your time, and your emotional and financial resources, and defend a petition? It will merely delay the inevitable; eventually you will have lived apart for five years and your partner will be able to rely on that fact.

One other very good reason not to defend a petition based on your partner's behaviour is that you are quite likely to respond with accusations in a tit-for-tat sort of way. These accusations can rebound and even prove the claims which have been made about you.

> One husband, who attempted to defend his wife's divorce petition based on his behaviour, claimed that his marriage had not broken down and that he wished for a reconciliation. He then proceeded to hoist himself with his own petard by describing his expectations about marriage to the court in such a way that it was absolutely clear that he was a chauvinist who had undermined his wife throughout the marriage and destroyed her self-esteem. He also maintained that she had only married him to get her hands on his money and property. The wife was granted a divorce.

If you are determined to defend the application, you must be able to challenge the accusations made about you, calmly and without retaliation. You must also be able to show that you realistically believe that the relationship can be salvaged, an almost impossible task if your partner believes otherwise.

Cross-petitions

You may wish to deny your partner's claims about the relationship yet want to end it, but on your terms. You may issue a cross-petition and ask the court to grant you a decree or order or a cross-decree or cross-order. You will find more information in Chapter 7.

4

Decrees and orders of nullity

A rare but important remedy

Decrees or orders of nullity are rare, and can only be granted in strictly limited circumstances. The majority of couples are likely to regard them as irrelevant. They remain important, however, for those few partners who are eligible to apply for them. Approximately 140 decrees of nullity are granted annually, but to date only one civil partner has obtained an order of nullity.

Marriage and civil partnerships are in effect contracts and are only valid if you satisfy certain requirements. If you have not done so, your relationship will be invalid and you will be eligible to apply for a decree or order of nullity. You will also be free to enter into a new legal relationship.

In recent years, nullity has become an important remedy for a number of young people from immigrant backgrounds who have been forced into marriage by their parents. It has allowed them to escape from a relationship to which they did not consent, and start afresh.

Nullity was also important for the model Jerry Hall, who went through a Hindu ceremony of marriage in Bali with the English pop singer Mick Jagger. The couple failed to register the ceremony with the authorities in Bali, as required by Balinese law. Their so-called marriage was, therefore, invalid. When their relationship broke down nine years later, Jerry Hall could not apply for a divorce because there was no relationship from which she could be divorced. Instead, she applied for a decree of nullity here, and it was granted. Had the decree not been available to her, she would not have been able to apply for a division of Mick Jagger's substantial property and financial assets.

Two forms of nullity: void and voidable relationships

There are two forms of nullity: the first makes a relationship void, and the second makes it voidable. The distinction between the two is not easy to understand but is very important for those who believe their relationships to be invalid because the grounds on which each is based, and the consequences, are very different.

Void relationships

No necessity to obtain a decree or order

A void relationship is one which never came into existence and, provided that you meet the requirements, it is not absolutely necessary for you to apply to court to obtain a nullity decree or order; you are free to marry or enter into a civil partnership without doing so.

Reasons to obtain a decree or order

The law, however, allows you to petition for a decree or order in the case of a void relationship if you wish to do so, for three reasons. First, it is recognized that even though your relationship is invalid, you may have entered into it in good faith and accepted financial responsibility for your partner, and acquired children. A decree or order permits you to make an agreement to divide your property or other assets and make arrangements for the future of your children, or let the court decide them for you (see Chapters 5 and 6). If you do not obtain a decree or order, you cannot take advantage of this.

Second, the law recognizes that you may prefer to make it clear to those who believe that you are in a valid relationship that you are not. Your friends and family who witnessed your 'marriage' or 'civil partnership' may not understand the law. It would be most unfortunate if they were to stand up and protest, just as you are about to marry or enter into a civil partnership with a new partner, that you are not free to do so.

Third, the law accepts that a person other than one of the partners may have good reasons for wanting to prove that a relationship is void. For example, you may have been given a right to inherit property under a will, provided you had married or entered into a civil partnership. Any person who would have inherited if you had not done so may apply for a decree or order of nullity of your relationship.

Examples of void relationships

A transsexual went through a ceremony of marriage with a woman without revealing his original gender; he had been born a female. The relationship was void because you may only marry a person of the opposite gender to your birth gender unless you have obtained a gender recognition certificate from a gender recognition panel. The 'husband' had not done so. He had no financial resources of his own and wanted to obtain the decree to allow him to apply for financial support from his wealthy 'wife'. The decree was granted, but his application for financial support was not. The court maintained that he had misled his 'wife' about his gender.

In 2007, a married woman and her lesbian lover attempted to register a civil partnership. The relationship was void, and the married woman was found guilty of perjury for lying to the registrar about her marital status. She maintained that she thought she could claim to be single because at the time of the registration her husband was planning to divorce her and that, for her, the registration was merely a sort of blessing. The court, not surprisingly, did not believe her. The woman resumed her relationship with her husband and became pregnant by him with their third child.

Voidable relationships

Voidable relationships are a little more common than void relationships. They are relationships which according to the law are potentially invalid. However, they do not actually become invalid until either partner with grounds to apply chooses to do so and is granted a decree or order.

You might be forgiven for finding it difficult to understand the difference between a voidable relationship and one which ends in divorce or dissolution, because they are so similar.

In the case of a voidable relationship, no one other than the partners may apply for a decree or order of nullity.

As in the case of void relationships, a decree or order allows you to make an agreement to divide your property or other assets and make arrangements for the future of your children, or let the court decide them for you.

Examples of voidable relationships

In 2008, Dr Humayra Abedin, a trainee doctor here, was lured back to Bangladesh by members of her family and held captive there by them for four months. She spent part of the time locked away in a mental asylum. Her family drugged her and forced her to marry. She was rescued and returned to this country where she was able to apply for a decree of nullity.

One of the most extreme examples of a voidable relationship was the marriage between a Polish woman and an English man. The woman had been sentenced to three years' imprisonment in Poland for anti-government activities. She feared for her health and her future after her release from prison. The man married her, having divorced his wife in order to do so, and brought her to England. She was granted a decree of nullity because the court accepted that she was forced to marry to escape imprisonment. The husband was able to remarry his first wife, but subsequently divorced her again and remarried the Polish woman.

Grounds for a void relationship

The grounds for void relationships for married couples and civil partners are very similar.

Spouses and void relationships

Your relationship will be void if:

- you have married one of the following people related to you:
  - your parent
  - your child
  - your adoptive parent
  - your adopted child
  - your former adoptive parent
  - your former adopted child
  - your grandparent
  - your grandchild
  - your uncle
  - your aunt
  - your niece
  - your nephew
  - your half-uncle
  - your half-aunt
  - your half-niece
  - your half-nephew
  - your brother
  - your sister
  - your half-brother
  - your half-sister;

- you married under the age of 16 or your spouse is under the age of 16;
- you did not conform with certain administrative requirements for the marriage;
- you married a person who was already married or in a civil partnership, or you were married or in a civil partnership;
- you married a person of the same sex.

The majority of void marriages have involved people who attempted to marry a person of the same sex, or who were already married, or who did not conform with the essential administrative requirements.

In spite of newspaper stories, it is exceptionally rare for close family members to attempt to enter into a legal relationship with each other. In 2008, the Independent peer Lord Alton claimed that he had heard from a High Court judge that he had dealt with a case of nullity involving twins who had been separated at birth and adopted. They had met each other in adult life and married without realizing that they were related. The story has never been proven.

Civil partners and void relationships

Your relationship will be void if at the time you registered your civil partnership:

- your civil partner was one of the following people related to you:
  - your parent
  - your child
  - your adoptive parent
  - your adopted child
  - your former adoptive parent
  - your former adopted child
  - your grandchild
  - your grandparent
  - your uncle
  - your aunt
  - your niece
  - your nephew
  - your half-uncle
  - your half-aunt
  - your half-niece
  - your half-nephew
  - your brother
  - your sister
  - your half-brother
  - your half-sister;

- your civil partner was one of the following people:
  - a child of a former civil partner
  - a child of a former spouse
  - a former civil partner of a grandparent
  - a former civil partner of a parent
  - a former spouse of a grandparent
  - a former spouse of a parent
  - a grandchild of a former civil partner
  - a grandchild of a former spouse;

  unless, at the time you registered the civil partnership, you were both over the age of 21, and the younger of you had never lived with the older person and been treated as his or her child before reaching the age of 18;
- your civil partner was a person of the opposite sex;
- you or your civil partner were already married or in a civil partnership;
- you or your civil partner were under the age of 16.

Grounds for a voidable relationship

There are slightly different requirements for married couples and civil partners who wish to claim that their relationship is voidable. The major difference is the absence of any mention of sexual conduct. You may remember that the government deliberately made no mention of same-sex sexual conduct in the Civil Partnership Act 2004.

Spouses and voidable relationships

You must be able to prove one of the following:
- that you, or your spouse, have been impotent since your marriage;
- that your spouse has deliberately refused to have sex with you since your marriage;
- that you or your spouse did not truly consent to the marriage because of force, mistake, unsound mind or 'other reason';
- that you or your spouse, although normally capable of giving consent, were suffering from a mental disorder at the time you married;
- that your spouse was suffering from a venereal disease when you married, and you were unaware of it;
- that your spouse was pregnant by another man when you married, and you did not know about it;
- that, when you married, your spouse did not tell you that he or she

had changed gender and had been granted a gender recognition certificate;

- that, after your marriage, you or your spouse changed gender and was granted an interim gender recognition certificate (see 'Useful addresses' for further information).

You must normally apply for the decree within three years of your marriage, unless you are claiming that you or your spouse have been impotent since your marriage or that your spouse has deliberately refused to have sex with you since then. If either of you have acquired an interim gender recognition certificate, you must apply for the decree within six months of receiving the certificate. The court may refuse to grant the decree if, knowing that you had grounds to apply for a decree, you led your spouse to believe that you would not do so, and that it would be unjust to your spouse to grant it.

The majority of decrees are granted for lack of consent.

Civil partners and voidable relationships

For your relationship to be voidable you must be able to prove that at the date you registered the civil partnership:

- you or your partner did not truly consent because of force, mistake, unsound mind or 'other reason';
- you or your partner, although normally capable of giving consent, were suffering from a mental disorder at the time you registered your relationship;
- your civil partner was pregnant and had not told you;
- your civil partner did not tell you that he or she had changed gender and been granted a gender recognition certificate; or
- after you registered your civil partnership, you or your civil partner changed gender and were granted an interim gender recognition certificate.

You must apply to the court within three years of the date on which you registered your civil partnership, or within six months of obtaining a gender recognition certificate. The court may refuse to grant the order if, knowing that you had grounds to apply for it, you led your partner to believe that you would not do so, and that it would be unjust to your partner to grant it.

Lack of consent for 'other reason'

The law mentions lack of consent for a reason other than force, mistake or unsound mind, but does not explain what that means. It may be that if you later discover some important fact about your partner, which goes to the heart of the relationship and existed at the time you married or became a civil partner but was not revealed to you, you may be able to claim that you did not consent for 'other reason'.

The facts which spring to mind include:

- Your spouse is gay.
- Your civil partner is heterosexual.
- Your spouse or civil partner has a serious drug or alcohol addiction.
- Your spouse or civil partner has a serious criminal record.
- Your spouse or civil partner has a communicable serious disease.
- Your spouse or civil partner has a former partner with children.
- Your spouse is unable to have children.

5

Property and financial matters

Property and finances do matter

When a relationship ends, property and financial matters are one of the biggest sources of discontent and disputes, and it is easy to understand why. You are surrounded by loss and uncertainty – even the family home and your means of support are at risk. Unfortunately, loss at the end of a relationship may be inevitable. One or both of you will usually have to make adjustments to your standard of living.

Even the super-rich suffer loss. After her well-publicized divorce from the wealthy musician Paul McCartney, Heather Mills, a charity campaigner and former model, had to accept that an award of £24 million would not allow her to enjoy her previous lifestyle. The actor and comedian John Cleese commented, after being forced to hand over £12.5 million to his former wife, 'In my 70th year I will still be spending two months a year doing work that is of no interest to me and which is probably slightly spiritually depleting in order to feed the beast.'

Dealing with the assets

Marriage and civil partnerships are normally entered into as a joint venture. Both partners contribute to the relationship and make sacrifices which have economic consequences for them and their children. Once a relationship has legally ended, it is necessary to divide the assets acquired during it: first, to maintain the partners, and second, to compensate them for the contribution and sacrifices they made during the relationship.

In this chapter, I will discuss the options open to you for dealing with the assets. I will not pretend that this topic is user-friendly, and you may find that you need to read it more than once to grasp its intricacies. Financial arrangements for children are, for the most part, treated separately in law, and will be considered in Chapter 6.

If you are wealthy, or have been in a relationship with a wealthy partner, or have complex property and financial affairs, you will need to consult an expert family lawyer, and probably a tax consultant, too, before you begin to think about how your assets should be divided.

Two options

There are two options for dealing with your assets. First, you may reach an agreement with your partner, draw up (or have your lawyer draw up) a legal document recording the details of the agreement, and ask the court to confirm it as a consent order. This order cannot be made before the legal end of your relationship; it will be enforceable in the same way as any other court order (see Chapter 7).

Second, if you are unable or unwilling to agree, you can apply to the court and let it decide for you. This second option is high-risk, because you will not necessarily get what you want. Your costs will be high and the process drawn out. It is not to be recommended and the majority of partners will do everything possible to reach an agreement.

Making an agreement with your partner

Before negotiating

Before you start any discussion with your partner, you may find it helpful to read the section below which explains how the court makes decisions about the division of relationship assets. It may centre your mind on the importance of negotiating with your partner, and persuade you that making an agreement would be a far preferable option to letting the court decide for you. Remind yourself of the importance of compromise. You cannot both get exactly what you want.

You may not find the idea of discussing property and financial matters with your partner easy to contemplate. Remember that you can always engage a mediator or collaborative lawyers to help negotiate an agreement (see Chapter 2).

Try to begin the discussions about the division of your assets well before the legal end of your relationship, even though the division cannot be legally implemented until the relationship has ended. You need to make plans for your future which will depend on your agreement.

If you believe that your partner's property and financial situation will improve in the near future, you may be tempted to delay your negotiations. Beware: the future is uncertain, and delaying can be a huge gamble on your part. Your partner's financial situation may worsen; new partners and new responsibilities may intervene, as may illness, or even death.

Make an inventory of everything you or your partner own or earn, and gather together any documents related to it. You should each draw up a budget. These will act as a starting point for your negotiations.

The negotiations

Homes, maintenance and pensions

The important concerns for most partners are where they will live and how they will maintain themselves, both in the immediate future and later in life (children, of course, are also a major concern but will be considered separately in Chapter 6).

A home for each of you You need to consider a number of related questions in your discussions about providing a home for each of you:

- Is there sufficient money for one of you to keep the family home? If so, which of you should that be?
- How will the other partner be housed?
- If one of you keeps the home, how will it be owned? Will it be owned by one of you outright, or will you continue to share ownership until the property is sold, on the occurrence of some future event? What will happen to the proceeds of sale?
- Who will be responsible for the maintenance of the property and mortgage payments?
- If the family home has to be sold, how will you each be rehoused?

Maintenance Both partners need to be able to fund their living costs, which will obviously depend on the resources available. If resources are plentiful, which is comparatively rare, any estimate of living costs should reflect the lifestyle you had during your relationship.

If either of you has a new partner or cohabitant who is making a financial contribution to your needs, you may want to consider whether that should be taken into account in that it reduces your living costs.

You will also want to take into account any child support payments (see Chapter 6) and any expenditure necessary because either of you has taken on additional obligations, perhaps for a new family or elderly relatives. These will all reduce the available financial resources.

If the resources are insufficient, you will need to consider how budgets can be cut or income increased. A partner who has been caring for family and home may find that he or she will now have to find work.

Pension funds and insurance policies If one of you has a pension fund, once it has been professionally valued it will be possible to split it to allow the partner without a pension fund to acquire one.

It is also possible for a portion of a pension fund to be 'earmarked'. This permits the transfer of the 'earmarked' portion to the partner who has no pension when the pension-owning partner retires.

Don't ignore insurance policies. You will need to discuss with the insurance company how best to continue with a policy in favour of a partner, or set up a new policy, after the relationship has legally ended.

Transferring the assets

Once you have agreed the division of the assets in a way which will house and maintain you, you need to consider whether you would prefer an outright transfer of your share of the family home or a lump sum payment. Either of these would allow you to make a clean break with each other. If the nature and amount of the assets permit it, this will normally be the preferred option. You will then be able to start your new life economically independent.

Periodical payments

If there are few or no capital assets but one partner has sufficient income, the only available option will be periodical payments. You may want to consider whether the payments can be secured against an asset of the partner making them (if there is such an asset available), or by way of a life insurance policy. The payments will then continue to be made in the event of a reduction in his or her income, or death. Other questions to discuss include whether the payments should be limited to a specific period of time, and in what circumstances they should be reviewed.

Remember that periodical payments are a high-risk option for both of you. They keep you locked into a relationship with each other. If you are the recipient, you will lose them in certain situations regardless of what you agreed with your former partner:

- If you remarry or enter into a new civil partnership, your former partner is likely to stop making the payments. If you have had the agreement confirmed in a consent order the court cannot enforce payments in these circumstances.
- If your former partner no longer has sufficient income to pay, unless the payments are secured against an asset he or she can ask the court to decrease the periodical payments or end them.
- If your former partner dies, you will lose the payments unless they are secured against an asset or a life insurance policy.

If you are the person making the payments and your circumstances improve, you risk your former partner going to court to ask for the consent order to be varied and the payments to be increased. The court may vary the payments or replace them with the transfer of a lump sum payment or other assets.

Sharing excess resources

Once you have made sure that each of you and the children can be housed and maintained, there may be few or no assets remaining. If there are, you might want to consider whether, and how, they should be shared. In some cases equal division of the remaining assets might be a fair solution to reflect the joint venture nature of your relationship (if that is what it was). You might like to consider the following matters to help you decide:

- The value of the assets: if they are substantial, you may feel that it would be unreasonable to divide them equally unless they are truly the product of a joint enterprise.
- The nature of the assets: how will you divide household goods?
- When were the assets acquired: before the relationship began, during it or after it ended? Should these be excluded from equal division?
- Were any assets inherited or are there personal gifts which should remain with their owner?

- By whose efforts, either direct or indirect, were the assets acquired?
- Did either of you make a truly exceptional contribution to the relationship, or to the creation of the assets, or sacrifice a career to allow your partner to be successful?
- Who is to be the prime carer for the children? Should the carer's ongoing contribution to family life, and the sacrifice involved, be taken into account?
- How long was your relationship?

No excess resources for sharing, but high income

Where there are no excess resources to be shared but one partner has a substantial income, you may wish to consider increasing the periodical payments for maintenance. This would fairly acknowledge the contribution and sacrifice made during the relationship by the other partner.

Drawing up the agreement

If your affairs are fairly straightforward and you and your former partner are able to cooperate, you may be able to draw up a document recording your agreement yourselves. Don't itemize every vegetable peeler, lemon zester or ball of string in the kitchen drawer which has become the repository for all those objects which have no other home.

If you do not want to draw up the agreement yourself, a lawyer will be able to do it for you. If your affairs are complex, you will probably have engaged a lawyer, and perhaps an accountant too, to negotiate and draw up your agreement for you.

The consent order

Court approval

Once the document recording your agreement has been completed, you or your lawyer should send it to the court for its approval. Remember that you cannot do this before your relationship has legally ended. If the court approves the agreement it will become a consent order, which is a formal order of the court and binding on you both.

Although the court can refuse to approve the agreement, it is rare for it to do so. The court has limited time, as well as minimal information about your circumstances. It will only refuse to approve your agreement if it is glaringly obvious that it would be unreasonable and unfair to either of you to do so.

Remarriage or a new civil partnership

If you have remarried or entered into a new civil partnership, you are considered to be the financial responsibility of your new partner. The court cannot confirm an agreement for periodical payments as a consent order. It may, however, confirm an agreement for the division of capital assets.

Overturning consent orders

Although either partner can ask the court to review periodical payments at a future date, neither may ask the court to review consent orders for the transfer of property or other capital assets, other than in cases of dishonesty or other very exceptional circumstances.

It is therefore important that you are honest with your former partner before you finalize your agreement. If you conceal any assets, or fail to reveal an intention to remarry or enter into a new civil partnership, you risk your former partner, on discovering the truth, returning to court to ask for the consent order to be overturned.

In very rare situations, the circumstances on which the consent order was based may change dramatically soon after the court granted the order. If so, you may return to court and ask for the consent order to be overturned.

> One couple agreed that the former wife should be given the family home and that there would be no further financial obligations between her and her husband. The court confirmed the agreement in a consent order. Five weeks later she killed her two children and committed suicide. She left all her property to her mother in her will. The former husband returned to court and succeeded in getting the consent order overturned.

Failure to obtain a consent order

If you make an agreement with your former partner but fail to have it approved by the court as a consent order, you take the risk that he or she might not abide by it and the court might not enforce it. It is always better to have your agreement confirmed as a consent order and avoid the worry of a challenge in the future.

Ancillary relief – letting the court decide

A quasi-lucky dip

Letting the court decide your ancillary relief is very high-risk, and I use the word 'risk' deliberately. The legal guidelines, which the court must use to make a decision, are very fuzzy indeed. They give an enormous amount of discretion to the judges, who interpret them in a way they believe will produce a fair result. Fairness, as you know, is in the eye of the beholder, and it is the judges' eyes we are talking about here. Your view of fairness and a judge's may differ greatly. You will have little idea in advance what order might be granted, and you may be very disappointed.

During your relationship, only those assets which you and your partner agreed should be jointly owned belong to both of you; the rest remain your individual property. When a relationship has legally ended and the partners place themselves in the hands of the court, it is uninterested in who owns what. It has the power to put all your assets into one large pot (or a small one if the assets are few) and decide who gets what. The process has been described as a quasi-lucky dip, and this is a very appropriate description.

Many couples who have been through this process believe that the outcome is unpredictable and depends entirely on the judge on the day. There is more than an element of truth in this belief, and there are even judges who share this view. This is hardly satisfactory and makes it very difficult for you to plan your future. Armed with this knowledge, you may decide to change your mind about letting the court decide, and return rapidly to the negotiating table.

Applications for ancillary relief

If you are the partner petitioning the court to end your relationship, you must state in your petition that you want to apply for ancillary relief, even though the court cannot consider this application before the legal end of your relationship. If you fail to do this and later change your mind, you will have to get the court's permission to make an application. Permission will not be given if you have remarried or entered into a new civil partnership. This is an important point to note, and as a petitioner you should always hedge your bets and make it clear in your petition that you want to apply for ancillary relief.

A respondent does not have to state an intention to apply for ancillary relief unless he or she defends the petition, in which case the intention is stated in the answer to the petition (see Chapter 7). In the majority of cases, the respondent will simply apply for ancillary relief once the relationship has legally ended.

If you are the petitioner, the court can consider your application for ancillary relief even if you have remarried or entered into a new civil partnership, provided that you stated an intention to apply for ancillary relief in the petition. However, it can only make an order for a transfer of property or other assets. It cannot make an order for periodical payments. The court will treat a respondent who applies for ancillary relief after he or she has entered into a new legal relationship in the same way.

If you are only cohabiting and apply for ancillary relief, the court may make orders for periodical payments in addition to orders for the transfer of property and other assets.

> In 2009, the court ordered a wealthy former husband to pay periodical payments of £125,000 a year to his former wife, who was pregnant by her new lover. The court's reasoning was that the man was not free to marry her, was not maintaining her, and the new relationship was not a stable one.

Courts are reluctant to make orders for ancillary relief if you delay your application for too long. It is generally seen as unfair to make a former partner hand over assets earned solely by his or her own efforts. An exception might be made if you delayed applying because there were insufficient assets to adequately compensate or maintain you when your relationship was legally ended.

Court orders for ancillary relief

The court has a very wide range of orders it can make in its redistribution of the assets. The orders are:

Interim maintenance payments

These are payments for maintenance until a final order for ancillary relief is made by the court.

Lump sum payments

These orders can be either for maintenance or to reflect your contribution to the relationship. They cannot be taken away from you except in exceptional circumstances (similar to the exceptional circumstances for overturning consent orders discussed on p. 54).

Periodical payments

The court can award periodical payments for maintenance, or to reflect your contribution to the relationship where there are insufficient assets to make a lump sum order. The payments may be secured against a capital asset (if there is one available) or an insurance policy. A court order for periodical payments has the same problems and carries the same risks as periodical payments agreed by the partners (see p. 51).

Property orders

In the majority of cases, property will consist of the family home.

Sale of property   Where resources are limited, the court may have little choice but to order the sale of the property and divide the proceeds in the best way possible to house each partner. If the division is insufficient to fund two homes, one or both partners will have to rent.

A right to live in the property   The court may make an order to allow one of you to live in the property until some future event, such as your children reaching the age of 18 or ending full-time education, or until the partner occupying the property remarries or enters into a new civil partnership, or dies. The court may also order what should happen to the property when that event occurs. It may, for instance, order the property to be returned to the partner who owns it, or sold and the proceeds divided between you.

The problem with this solution is that if you are the one who remains in the property, you may be lured into a false sense of security and fail to confront the fact that this is a short-term solution. You could find it quite destabilizing when you eventually have to move.

Outright transfer   If there are sufficient resources to house each partner, the court may transfer the property outright to one partner. If there is a mortgage over the property, the court can decide who should pay it.

Transfer of a lease   If you rent your family home, the court can order the lease to be transferred from one partner to the other.

Pension orders

The court may make an attachment order which ensures that all or part of a pension may be 'earmarked', and transferred on the pension owner's retirement to his or her former partner.

A more satisfactory order is for the court to order the immediate transfer of a portion of a pension. This can be used by the recipient to build up a pension in his or her own right.

These pension orders are not available following a decree or order of judicial separation. They are not needed on separation because you retain your status of spouse or civil partner for pension purposes.

Variation of marriage or civil partnership settlements

Marriage or civil partnership settlements are not defined in law and can cover any type of arrangement which has been set up by the partners, or their parents or relatives, either before or during the relationship, for the benefit of the family. The court may alter the terms of a settlement. Such settlements are generally used for tax purposes and are fairly uncommon.

How the courts decide

When deciding the type and amount of any order, the courts must take into account all the circumstances of the case and, in particular, the following matters specifically laid down by law.

Children

Of first importance is the welfare of any child. Children here include not only your biological and adopted children, but also any other child for whom either of you is responsible and who has lived with you as part of your family. The court has limited powers to make financial orders for children since the Child Support Act came into existence (see Chapter 6 for more details). Children's needs, such as childcare, can be taken into account by the court in making an order for the parent who will be caring for them in the future.

The clean break principle

Wherever possible, the court will try to make it possible for you and your former partner to put the past behind you and begin your life apart financially independent of each other and unable to make further future claims. This is known as the clean break principle.

All your assets

In theory, all your assets are available for court orders. However, the court can exclude certain types of assets in the interests of fairness. Of course, if your assets are limited, the court will have to include all of them, regardless of their source.

Assets which may be excluded:

- *Assets generated by one partner*: in truly exceptional cases, the court may exclude assets earned solely by the activities of one partner. Normally, it will not do so for fear of penalising home-makers who have often made an indirect contribution to the creation of the assets. As one Law Lord put it so graphically, 'The cock-bird can feather his nest precisely because he is not required to spend most of his time sitting on it.'

- *Assets acquired before the relationship began*: you may find that the courts will exclude assets which one of you purchased before the marriage or registration of a civil partnership, unless it is property which subsequently became the family home.
- *Gifts and inherited assets*: the court will try to exclude gifts made to one partner, or assets inherited by one partner.
- *Compensation awarded for personal injuries*: compensation given to a partner for personal injuries is for his or her personal use.
- *Assets acquired after the breakdown or legal end of your relationship*: you may have acquired assets after the breakdown or legal end of your relationship. If they relate in some way to the relationship, the court may be prepared to include them. The longer the time between the breakdown, or legal end of your relationship, and your application for ancillary relief, the less likely it is that the court will include this type of asset.

Needs and standard of living during the relationship

For the majority of former partners, the available assets will only cover essential needs such as housing, food, clothing and transport. If, however, the assets are substantial, the court may take into account the standard of living you enjoyed during the relationship in calculating your needs.

If your former partner is receiving financial contributions towards his or her maintenance from a cohabitant, those contributions can be taken into account and may reduce the court's assessment of his or her needs. The cohabitant can often view this as an indirect contribution to a former partner and feel somewhat resentful.

Obligations

Obligations include maintaining a member of your extended family for whom you are responsible, or a new partner or cohabitant, or children of your new family. Former partners applying for ancillary relief often regard this as unfair because these obligations reduce the amount available for their needs.

Age

Age may be a relevant factor if it prevents either of you from working, or if either of you have special age-related needs.

Length of the relationship

The courts have tended to be generous to former partners whose relationships have lasted a long time. It is more likely that they have made a significant contribution to the relationship. Occasionally, a partner in a short relationship may receive a sizeable award because his or her contribution was viewed as important.

> Heather Mills maintained that her contribution to her marriage to Paul McCartney had been exceptional. She told the court that she had been his full-time wife, mother, lover, confidante, business partner and psychologist, who had helped him recover from the death of his first wife and given him back his confidence to perform again. She claimed that her suggestion that he should wear an acrylic fingernail, because he had worn down a fingernail on his left hand to the extent that it bled when he played his guitar, was an important factor in helping his career. She also claimed that she helped design sets and lighting for his concerts. The judge regarded her claims as 'hyperbolic make-believe and devoid of any reality', and awarded her £24.3 million of her former husband's £440 million fortune. The award was primarily based on her, and their daughter's, reasonable needs.

Disability

Disability of a partner will only be relevant if it requires specific expenditure.

> The court refused to make one former wife pay maintenance to her former husband who had become severely disabled because of his alcoholism. He was cared for by his parents, and had few needs which were not already being met. His former wife was not well off and had suffered during the marriage because of his alcoholism.

Contribution to the welfare of the family now or in the future

If you have taken care of your family or will be taking care of them in the future, particularly at the expense of your career, it may be taken into account.

> The former wife of footballer Ray Parlour was given periodical payments of £406,500 per year, to be reviewed after four years. She had helped him get his career back on track. There were insufficient assets to make a lump sum order.

Conduct, if it would be unfair to disregard it

The courts hate judging conduct and have made clear that they will only take into account truly exceptional good or bad conduct.

> One husband attacked his wife with knives in front of their children. He was convicted of attempted murder and sent to prison for 12 years. The

wife was so traumatized by the serious wounds to her neck, hands and face that she was unable to work. The court redistributed the assets, giving £300,000 to the wife and £30,000 to the husband.

Another 'husband', a transsexual, was denied ancillary relief after a decree of nullity. The court judged his conduct to be seriously blameworthy. His 'wife' maintained that he had hidden his gender change from her for 15 years. It is a little hard to believe that she was without blame; she maintained that she had never seen her 'husband' naked, and she had received donor insemination to conceive their two children.

The potential loss of any benefit because your relationship was legally ended

This type of loss might include any assets earned by your partner during the relationship but which will not be realized until some time in the future. Bonuses or shares, for example, may come into this category.

An inheritance promised under a will is not such a benefit because a will can be changed at any time before death.

The importance of fairness

It is not surprising that the judges have found it difficult to decide ancillary relief applications when the law has given them so many factors to take into account. In recent years, they have decided to stress the importance of fairness. The emphasis on fairness is based on the view that marriage and civil partnerships are joint ventures, and when they end:

- the needs of both partners must be met;
- any contribution, domestic or otherwise, which either partner made to the relationship should be recognized and compensated for;
- any loss which either partner suffered as a result of the relationship should be compensated for.

One can only be sympathetic towards the judges; they have an impossible task. However, by adding this requirement of fairness, their task, and your understanding of the process of ancillary relief, has probably not been made any easier.

Equal division of the assets – a starting point

There is a popular assumption that once the court has satisfied itself that all your needs have been met, it will divide the remainder of the assets created during the relationship equally. Remember, this is only the court's starting point; it will take into account all the matters discussed above before making a final decision.

If the assets are extremely high, it is doubtful whether they will ever be divided equally, unless they were created by both partners in a joint business venture.

> Beverly Charman, the wife of the wealthy insurance broker John Charman, was awarded £48 million after a 30-year marriage, the highest order ever made in the UK. Yet it did not represent half of her husband's £130 million fortune. The courts seem reluctant to deprive the very wealthy of half their assets if their former partners' needs and contribution to the relationship can be generously met with less.

Pre-relationship agreements and applications for ancillary relief

If you made an agreement with your partner, before your marriage or civil partnership, to deal with your property and other assets in the event that your relationship should end, don't rely on it when your relationship has been legally ended. The problem with these agreements is that it is not possible to have them confirmed by a consent order at the time they are made, and there is nothing to prevent your partner applying to the court for ancillary relief.

The courts have been remarkably reluctant to take these agreements into account when deciding applications for ancillary relief. The view is that when you signed it, the future was unknown. By the time the relationship ended, you may have given up a career to have children or taken on other family responsibilities which were not foreseen at the time of the agreement. To enforce an agreement which would leave one of you homeless and without financial resources and perhaps dependent on the state would be most unfair.

Signs of change

Change is afoot: there are a number of cases where the courts have agreed to enforce all, or part, of a pre-relationship agreement when an application for ancillary relief has been made. The courts have taken into account whether the couple took legal advice before signing the agreement, whether there was any undue pressure on a partner to sign, and whether it would be fair in all the circumstances to enforce it and refuse to make an order for ancillary relief.

A recent example

In 2009, the court considered a pre-nuptial agreement in the well-publicized case of Katrin Radmacher, a wealthy German heiress, and Nicolas

Granatino, an investment banker from a wealthy French background. The couple met at a nightclub in London, and on their engagement Katrin's father persuaded her to have a pre-nuptial agreement drawn up to protect her £150 million fortune. Nicolas agreed that he would make no claim against Katrin if they were to divorce. The agreement was legally enforceable in their home countries. The couple married in England in 1998. When their marriage broke down in 2006, they had two daughters. Nicolas had left his job and become an Oxford academic earning £30,000 per year. He applied to the court for ancillary relief and Katrin asked for their agreement to be enforced.

The court partly enforced the agreement and partly granted Nicolas' application for ancillary relief. He received a £100,000 lump sum and £2.5 million with which to buy a house to live in until the younger of his daughters was 22; the house would then go back to Katrin. She also agreed to pay £700,000 of his £800,000 debts.

The court took into account that the couple knew what they were doing when they signed the agreement and were aware that such agreements were enforceable in their home countries.

Nicolas has appealed to the Supreme Court maintaining that he will be financially ruined if he does not receive a better settlement. The court's decision is expected shortly.

Enforcement of court orders

The majority of former partners usually comply with court orders, including consent orders, for ancillary relief. If they do not, there are a number of options for enforcement:

- *Attachment of earnings*: the court can order your former partner's employer to deduct payments from his or her salary and pay them to the Central Attachment of Earnings Payment System (CAPS), from where they will be sent to you on a regular basis. This is perhaps the most powerful means of enforcement.
- *Payment by standing order*: the court can demand that your former partner make payments to you by standing order. It can also order your former partner to open a bank account if he or she does not have one.
- *Charging order*: this is an order made by the court which imposes a charge on one of your former partner's assets. Once this has happened, you may then apply to the court for the asset to be sold and the proceeds to be paid to you.
- *A judge may sign documents of transfer*: if the court makes an order

transferring an asset to you, and your former partner refuses to sign the relevant documents to make the transfer, you may ask the judge to sign instead.

- *Debts owed to your former partner*: if your former partner is owed money, you may ask the court to order that the money be paid directly to you. This may be done via your former partner's bank account. The bank can be ordered to freeze the account until there are sufficient funds to pay you. This method cannot be used to enforce periodical payments.
- *Prison*: your former partner can be ordered to explain to the court, in person, his or her failure to comply with a court order. If the court believes the non-compliance was deliberate, it can order a prison sentence for contempt of court. The power is rarely used.

State financial support

If there are insufficient financial resources for ancillary relief, you may be forced to rely on state support. In these circumstances, it is worth applying to the court for nominal periodical payments. This will allow you to return to court if your former partner acquires resources in the future.

Do not feel embarrassed about applying for state benefits. They are available precisely to help those who find themselves in financial difficulty, more often than not through no fault of their own. The benefits may well help you to move towards financial independence.

State support includes many different types of benefits, some means-tested and others not. You should contact your local benefits office for up-to-date information on the benefits available and your eligibility to claim them (see 'Useful addresses').

If you are eligible for state benefits, you may also be able to claim further help to pay the interest on any mortgage or loan, or the rent on your home, and council tax.

Remember that if you have remarried or entered into a new civil partnership, or are cohabiting, your new partner's or cohabitant's income will be taken into account in assessing your eligibility for any means-tested benefits. Whether you are actually being financially supported is irrelevant.

Bankruptcy

Bankruptcy is a legal option for those who are unable to pay their debts. The trustee in bankruptcy takes charge of the bankrupt's assets, if any, and redistributes them among the creditors to discharge the debts and give the bankrupt a clean financial slate. Bankruptcy is not unusual when a relationship breaks down. The stress of the breakdown may have precipitated the bankruptcy, or the stress of the bankruptcy may have been the cause of the breakdown.

You should watch out for the possibility of bankruptcy, and try to make sure that all ancillary relief matters are finalized before it happens.

If you suspect that your former partner is not really insolvent but is trying to use the bankruptcy to maliciously thwart your application for ancillary relief, you can apply to the court to have the bankruptcy annulled.

You should always obtain professional legal advice from a family or insolvency lawyer if your partner has filed for bankruptcy, or you fear might do so.

Bankruptcy before a court order for ancillary relief

If your former partner files for bankruptcy before you have obtained a court order for ancillary relief, all his or her assets will go to the trustee in bankruptcy. There will be nothing left for you. In this case, it is important that you know who owns what. If the family home is in both your names, the trustee in bankruptcy can only take your partner's share, and you may be allowed to buy that share at market value.

Despite the bankruptcy, it may still be worthwhile applying for ancillary relief. The court can make an order for the transfer of any assets which will be available at the end of the bankruptcy. It can also make an order for nominal periodical payments. Once your partner is discharged from bankruptcy, if he or she has assets you may apply to the court for an increase in the periodical payments. You may also ask for them to be replaced by an order to transfer property or other assets to you.

Bankruptcy after a consent order or other court order

Once the court has made an order for your ancillary relief, and property, or other asset, has been transferred, the subsequent bankruptcy of your former partner cannot affect it.

If the property, or asset, has not actually been transferred when the bankruptcy happens, the order becomes a debt against the bankrupt and takes second place to all the other debts. However, unlike other debts, ancillary relief orders can be enforced after the bankrupt has been discharged from bankruptcy.

If you have been awarded periodical payments by the court before the bankruptcy happens, and your former partner is earning, the trustee in bankruptcy can allow your basic needs to be met from the bankrupt's earnings before using them to pay off the debts.

Once your former partner has been discharged from bankruptcy, your periodical payments will be resumed in full and you may also claim for any shortfall in them which occurred during the bankruptcy.

Inheritance

During your marriage or civil partnership, you may inherit from your partner if you have been named in the will. If there is no will, you have a legal right to a fixed share of your partner's estate (see p. 14).

Once your relationship has legally ended, you will lose any right to inheritance even if your former partner has not removed your name from the will. You will also lose your legal right to inherit a fixed share in the absence of a will. The only exception to this is if you have been granted a decree of judicial separation or a separation order. Then your right to inherit will continue, provided that you have not been removed from your partner's will. You will, however, lose your legal right to inherit a fixed share in the absence of a will.

The law allows former partners the right to apply to the court for support from a deceased former partner's estate. However, the majority of court orders, including consent orders, will normally include a clause removing this right on the assumption that the order has fairly redistributed the assets.

It is important that you make a new will after the legal end of your relationship. If you decide that you want your former partner to inherit from you, you must make that intention clear.

Legal costs

Beware escalation

If you are planning to engage a lawyer and other experts to negotiate an ancillary agreement with your former partner for you, try not to wrangle over trivialities. Remind yourself regularly that the costs of endless meetings with lawyers, together with letters, emails and telephone calls, will be expensive.

If you have to apply to court for ancillary relief, your lawyer's costs will be even higher and may well use up a significant proportion of the assets. One judge compared the costs in ancillary relief disputes to those in the well-known case of *Jarndyce* v. *Jarndyce* in Charles Dickens' novel *Bleak House*, which ate up all of the parties' inheritance.

Each partner is normally responsible for his or her own costs. However, if you behave unreasonably during the ancillary relief process, the court can order you to pay all the costs.

Legal aid

If you need help with legal costs because you are on a low income or receiving state benefits, or have minimal capital, you may be eligible for government-funded legal aid. This is organized by the Legal Services Commission (LSC) and has a helpline, Community Legal Advice. If you are eligible, you will be able to get free legal advice from a lawyer who has a contract with the LSC. If you need a lawyer to represent you in court, permission has to be obtained from the LSC, who will decide whether your request is a reasonable one.

Remember that not all lawyers offer a legal aid service and it can be difficult to find one who does (see 'Useful addresses' for further information on the LSC helpline and how to find a legal aid lawyer).

The statutory charge

Legal aid is not free money. If the court grants you a share of your partner's property or other assets, or allows you to keep assets which belong to you by refusing to give your partner a share of them, you will normally have to repay the legal aid. You can delay repayment of this debt if you have insufficient capital and the asset given to you, or retained by you, is the family home or will be used to purchase one. If you sell that property and buy another family home, repayment can also be delayed. The debt will be registered as a statutory charge on your new property to make sure that you cannot sell the property without repaying the money owed. Once you have paid the debt, the charge is lifted from your home.

Where the asset is used for purposes other than a family home, and in very limited circumstances, you may not have to repay the legal aid if it would cause you serious hardship; your lawyer will be able to advise you on this matter.

If your partner is ordered to pay your legal costs, you will not have to repay legal aid.

6

Your children's best interests

Relationship breakdown and its effect on children

Christopher, a four-year-old, on being told that his parents were getting divorced asked his mother, 'When parents get divorced, do they kill the children?'

Children's minds work in a very different way from those of adults, as illustrated by Christopher's poignant and scary question. After all, if their parents whom they love can get rid of each other, why would they not get rid of their children too? Many children of all ages are terrified at the thought of their parents leaving each other, even if they do not ask the same question as Christopher.

Parental killing of children, although not entirely unheard of, is exceptional. One father, in a state of depression about his forthcoming divorce, collected his children for a weekend visit and asphyxiated them, and himself, in his car. But tragedies like this are fortunately rare.

What is common is short-term psychological damage to children, and it would be unrealistic not to expect it. The loss of even an inadequate parent and the upheaval involved in reconstructing a new life will have some negative effects on your children. All responsible

68

parents will want to protect their children in so far as is possible. You may not always understand how to do this, and it can be hard if you are feeling emotionally fragile. At the end of this chapter there are some suggestions to help you minimize the damage to your children.

Agreeing your children's future

Cooperation, sensitivity and flexibility

One of the most important things you can do for your children is to cooperate with your partner and reach an agreement about all the important practical aspects of their future, including their financial support. If you cannot agree you will have to let the court decide, which could be distressing for you all, as well as costly.

When trying to reach an agreement, you should keep your children's best interests in mind and listen carefully to what they say if they are old enough to make their wishes known. It is perhaps not a good idea to make rigid decisions for children over the age of 16; they will ultimately vote with their feet if they do not like the decisions you have made.

Try to keep a balance between making firm plans and remaining flexible; both have their place. Some matters are best left to the good sense of each parent as and when they arise. Circumstances can change, and children's needs change with age.

Parental responsibility

Before you consider the details of agreements about your children's future, it may help you to understand the meaning of parental responsibility and who has it.

The meaning of parental responsibility

'Parental responsibility' is the term the law uses to cover all the rights and duties which parents have in relation to their children under the age of 18, and their property. It ends if a child marries or becomes a civil partner between the ages of 16 and 18. The precise rights and duties of parents are not clear but it is assumed that they normally include:

- contact with your children;
- making decisions about their living arrangements and upbringing;
- choosing their name, religion and education;
- caring for their assets;

- deciding their medical treatment, unless they are competent enough to decide for themselves.

Who has parental responsibility?

Married partners　If you are the biological parents of a child, or have jointly adopted a child, you will both have parental responsibility. If you have given birth to a child after fertility treatment in a licensed clinic with your husband's agreement, or if you have a joint parental order for a child conceived by way of surrogacy, you will also have joint parental responsibility.

A husband is presumed to be the biological father of any child conceived during the marriage unless he can prove otherwise. If you are not the biological father, you are in reality a step-parent, and may obtain parental responsibility by entering into a Parental Responsibility Agreement with your step-child's parents, or by applying to court for a Parental Responsibility Order.

Civil partners　If your partner had a child for whom he or she has parental responsibility, you are the step-parent of that child, and may acquire parental responsibility in the same way as any married step-parent.

If you jointly adopted a child, you and your partner will both have parental responsibility. If you are a lesbian partner and have given birth to a child after fertility treatment in a licensed clinic with the agreement of your partner, she will have joint parental responsibility with you. If you have had a child by way of surrogacy and were granted a joint parental order, you will also both have parental responsibility.

The agreement – matters to consider

The list below suggests the main issues you might like to consider when making an agreement.

Living arrangements

Probably the most important decision to make is with whom your children should live. This is likely to be determined by their age, who has been their main carer up to now, your work schedules, and whose home can best accommodate them. If both parents will be living in the same area and will have adequate accommodation for them, it may be possible for older children to divide their time between both parents. Not all children will be happy with this; they may find moving backwards and forwards unsettling, particularly in the immediate period after their parents have split up.

Contact

Children have a right to regular contact with both parents and it should not be bargained over. Do not use decisions about contact as ammunition in any war between yourself and your partner.

Arrangements about contact will depend on the age of the children and how far apart you live. Very young children may be happier with short periods of time away from their resident parent rather than long ones. If you live a long way from your former partner it may not be possible for children to visit frequently, and longer visits may be necessary as soon as they are old enough to cope with them. Who will deliver and collect the children if they cannot travel alone?

Do take care that the non-resident parent does not always have the children at weekends and holiday times. This can be difficult for the children because they may lose out on participation in team sports and other out-of-school activities, or seeing friends. Non-resident parents may need to have some free time at weekends or holiday time for their own activities, and resident parents may like to have time with the children when they are free from the constraints of school.

Important days of the year often take on a greater significance when the children have to share them between you and their other parent. Do decide how to divide contact for occasions such as birthdays, Christmas, Hanukah, Divali or Eid.

General upbringing

You should try to agree on your general expectations about your children's behaviour and social life. Try not to dictate to the other parent about what they are allowed to eat (unless for medical reasons), bedtime or computer and television time. It may be better to discuss these issues if a problem arises.

Medical treatment

You will both need to consent to any medical treatment for your children unless they are able to consent for themselves. In a medical emergency, the parent who is caring for the children at the time will clearly make any immediate decision. The other parent should be contacted as soon as possible if further consents are necessary.

Name

A child's name should not normally be changed, and both parents would have to agree to any proposed change. Problems can arise when the resident parent remarries or enters into a new civil partnership and decides to take the name of the new partner. If the child is very young, it can happen that he or she becomes commonly known by the step-parent's name, and accepts it.

Religion

There will be little problem over the religious future of your children if you both have the same religious beliefs, or none. Otherwise, you must decide how important it is to either of you for your children to be brought up in one particular faith, and in which religious rituals they should participate.

Education

If your children are in state schools, you may have little choice about where they will be educated. If there is a choice, it will be necessary for both of you to decide the matter. If they are to be privately educated, you will have to agree which school they are to attend.

Decide how information about school events, such as parents' evenings, concerts, plays, games, school reports, will be given to the non-resident parent and who will attend these events. Who will decide about children's participation in school trips?

Passports and other important documentation

If your children already have passports, you should decide who should take care of them along with any other important documents. The parent who does not have the originals should have copies of them. If your children do not have passports, you need to consider whether you will both agree to sign any application for a passport. It is possible for one parent to apply, but the other parent may contact the passport office and object.

Care of a child's assets

Decisions about assets will only be relevant in a limited number of cases. In most situations, children's assets will be held by trustees. If not, you will have to decide which of you is to be responsible for dealing with them.

Moving home

You may want to consider what should happen if one parent wishes to move a significant distance away, and the implications for contact and travel responsibilities.

If you wish to take a child under 16 abroad for longer than one month, you will require the consent of the other parent.

Consent to marriage or civil partnership

Both your consents are needed if your child wishes to marry or enter into a civil partnership under the age of 18.

Funeral arrangements

You may prefer not to deal with such matters in your agreement but you should be aware that both parents are normally responsible for a child's funeral arrangements.

Review of the agreement

Think about the circumstances which might make you want to review the agreement. Your children's needs or your own situations can change, and it could be appropriate for the roles of the resident and non-resident parent to be reversed at some point.

Enforceability of agreements

If your former partner were to decide not to abide by the agreement, you would have to go to court and the agreement would not necessarily be enforced. The court is legally bound to consider the welfare of the children when considering making an order affecting any aspect of their lives.

You may question the point of making an agreement about your children if such an agreement is not enforceable. Remember, however, that agreements are to help you and your former partner to cooperate and make life better for your children; they should be self-policing.

At the very least, try to centre your mind on the fact that if you do not make an agreement, you will have to let the courts decide for you. You may not get what you want, and it will delay the legal ending of your relationship (see Chapter 7).

We cannot agree – let the court decide

Court orders

If the court makes an order for your children, it will inevitably restrict some aspects of one partner's parental responsibility. You will only be able to act as permitted by the order. If you are a step-parent and did not already have parental responsibility, you may acquire certain aspects of parental responsibility as a result of the order.

The court will not normally make orders for children over 16 because it would be difficult to enforce them.

If you disobey a court order, you will be in contempt of court and may be sent to prison, although courts have shown a reluctance to do this; it punishes children as much as parents.

The court may make any of the following orders:

Residence orders

These orders decide with which parent the children should live; it is possible for shared residence to be ordered if appropriate.

Contact orders

These orders determine the type of contact, and how much, the children will have with their non-resident parent. If a parent is known to behave in a way which puts children at risk, the court may order supervised or indirect contact. Indirect contact means that a parent may only contact children by letter, email or possibly telephone.

Contact orders can be difficult to enforce. Resident parents have used an abundance of excuses to prevent contact, including: 'I was ill'; 'I forgot'; 'I had to go away'; 'The children were ill'; 'The children had school events'; or 'The children refuse to visit.' Unless you are prepared to go back to court over and over again, you may have to accept limited contact until the children are old enough to make decisions for themselves.

Prohibited steps orders

These orders prevent a parent from exercising a specific aspect of parental responsibility without the court's permission. For instance, the court can make an order restricting contact with the non-resident parent where it is damaging to a child.

Specific issue orders

The court may order a parent to exercise a specific aspect of parental responsibility. You may apply for this type of order if your former partner has refused to cooperate with a request from you relating to such matters as arranging medical treatment or attending a particular school.

Child abduction

Non-resident parents may be tempted to abduct their children from the care of the resident parent, particularly if they live abroad or have family there. If abduction is a strong possibility, you should act immediately and apply for a court order. You should try to keep the children's passports in your possession. If your children do not have passports, you should notify the passport office so that passports will not be issued for them without your consent. It is, of course, possible that the children have foreign passports, and you would need a court order for these to be put into the safe keeping of a lawyer or other responsible person.

If the abduction is an immediate risk, you should also contact the police, who will be able issue a warning to all points of departure from the UK.

Wardship

If you are afraid that your children are in any form of immediate danger from their other parent, you may apply to have them made wards of court. There is always a judge on duty to deal with such matters in an emergency. Once children have been made wards of court, they are in the care of the court and neither parent, nor any other person, can take any action concerning them without the court's permission.

Children's applications for orders

Children may apply for orders themselves but must first obtain the consent of the court. This may be helpful for children who wish to be cared for by another appropriate adult rather than a parent, or would like to have contact with relations, or brothers and sisters from whom they have been separated.

Step-parents and a child of the family

Step-parents often develop a very close relationship with their partners' children and are reluctant to lose that when they leave their partner. If you are a step-parent, even one who has not acquired parental responsibility (see p. 70), you may still be eligible to apply for court orders for your step-children if they lived with you during the relationship and you treated them as a member of your family.

How the court decides orders

One well-known family court judge has explained that,

> The courts recognize the critical importance of the role of both parents in the lives of their children. The courts are not anti-father and pro-mother or vice versa. The court's task . . . in every case is to treat the welfare of the child or children concerned as paramount, and to safeguard and promote the welfare of every child to the best of its ability.

Unless there are cogent reasons against it, the children of separated parents are entitled to know and have the love and society of both their parents. In particular, the courts recognize the vital importance of the role of non-resident fathers in the lives of their children, and only make orders terminating contact when there is no alternative.

Specific matters

The court must consider:

- children's feelings and wishes if they are old enough to understand the implications;
- children's physical and emotional needs;
- the potential effect on children of an order;
- the children's age, sex and background;
- any harm the children have suffered or might suffer;
- the parents', or any other person's, abilities to meet the children's needs.

Fathers and the court

The courts have had a tendency to give residence orders to mothers, particularly if the children are young. Recently, there has been a slight increase in residence orders in favour of fathers where they have shown themselves to be more able to meet their children's needs.

In 2009, the law firm Mishcon de Reya revealed the results of a survey of relationship breakdown over 20 years. It showed that 38 per cent of children never saw their father again after their parents' relationship ended.

Domestic violence and contact

Where a resident parent has accused a non-resident parent of domestic violence, the court will consider the allegation and, if proven, its effect on the children's physical and psychological well-being. Supervised contact can be ordered to take place in the non-resident parent's home or in a special contact centre. Indirect contact by means of letters, cards and presents can be ordered to keep the lines of communication open and permit a relationship in the future if appropriate. It is rare for contact to be denied completely.

Moving abroad

If the resident parent wishes to take the children to live abroad, contact will be difficult for the non-resident parent. In deciding whether to permit it, the court will take into account why the parent wishes to move and its potential effect on the children. Where the resident parent is unhappy and is moving back 'home' to be closer to family and a familiar culture, the court is likely to allow the children to leave because it is better for them to live with a happy parent than an unhappy one. The court will not permit the move if the motives for it are trivial or spiteful towards the non-resident parent.

Parental alienation syndrome

The court is particularly concerned about parental alienation syndrome. This is where a resident parent, primarily a mother, tries to turn the children against the non-resident parent to such an extent that the children refuse all contact. The resident parent may be doing it to exact revenge, or because he or she is insecure and afraid that the children might prefer to live with their non-resident parent.

It is not easy to prove that a parent is deliberately brainwashing children, and courts are reluctant to order children who object to have contact with their non-resident parent. In these circumstances, the courts may order indirect contact, to keep the relationship open and allow the children to realize that the non-resident parent has not abandoned them.

If the court believes that a resident parent has deliberately tried to alienate the children from their non-resident parent over a long period of time, it may order the children to live with the non-resident parent. Ultimately, the court could order the imprisonment of the resident parent for contempt of court.

If you believe that the resident parent is attempting to alienate your children, you should take prompt action. The longer you do not have contact with your children, the more difficult it will be to re-establish a relationship with them.

If you are accused of alienating your children and you have very good reason to believe that they are genuinely at risk of abuse from the non-resident parent, you should seek help immediately, and obtain as much evidence as possible to present to the court.

In 2009, the court ordered a secondary-school-age boy, against his will, to live with his father. They had had minimal contact with each other since the boy was two years old. The mother had persistently tried to alienate her son from his father and thwarted contact arrangements. The court's decision was based on the evidence of a child psychiatrist that the boy was being damaged emotionally by his mother's behaviour.

Financial support: a child's right, not a parental option

Children are perhaps the most expensive luxury of any relationship and continue to be so even when your relationship is over. They require significant funding to meet their seemingly never-ending needs. Financial support is a child's right and is not optional for parents. Most parents willingly undertake to support their children; they love them and want them to flourish and grow into successful happy adults. Unfortunately, once a relationship is over, financial support can be the source of serious resentment and conflict and may even be used as a bargaining tool for contact by a non-resident parent. Remember, even if you have little contact, your children still need to be maintained.

If either of you have a new partner and have taken on additional financial commitments, your children's needs must still be met. You cannot expect new partners to take over your responsibility for your children.

Compensation for resident parents

Maintenance payments for children do not include compensation to the resident parent for caring for the children even though he or she may have had to make career sacrifices to do so. Any compensation due should have been reflected in the agreement or court award for ancillary relief, if there were sufficient resources (see Chapter 5).

Types of financial arrangements

Financial arrangements for children fall into three categories:

● parental agreements
● Child Support Agency arrangements
● court orders.

Parental agreements for financial support

These are the gold standard for children; they are readily made by parents who acknowledge that, although their relationship is over, they remain committed to the financial support of their children.

When negotiating any agreement, keep the well-being of your children firmly in your mind. Negotiations should not be used to exact revenge on each other. Be honest with each other about your financial resources and draw up a realistic budget for your children's needs. Remember that any agreement must provide for maintenance payments to the resident parent which would not be less than you would have to pay after an assessment by the Child Support Agency (see p. 82).

Once you have reached an agreement, you should have it confirmed by the court as a legally enforceable consent order (see Chapter 7).

A word of warning – the 12-month rule

This rather unfortunate rule allows parents who have agreed their children's maintenance to end the agreement, once it has been in force for 12 months, and make an application to the Child Support Agency. The rule is often used as a bargaining weapon by a non-resident parent to get a resident parent to agree to a drop in maintenance payments or risk an assessment by the Agency, which could also reduce the level of payments.

Matters to consider when making an agreement

Your financial resources

Your children are a joint venture; if the resident parent has financial resources, it is reasonable to take them into account in deciding how much the non-resident parent should contribute. Do be realistic about the resources available for child support; parents have to live too.

If resources allow it, your children's standard of living should be similar to what it was during the relationship. If resources are limited, one or both parents will have to make efforts to increase income or reduce outgoings.

Shared residence

Where residence is shared between both parents, your agreement should reflect the amount of time the children spend with each of you.

Provision of property

Where the non-resident parent has provided housing for the resident parent and children, it should be reflected in the amount of maintenance payable.

Your children's needs

You should list all your children's needs; a computer spreadsheet is a good way of doing this as it can be updated to reflect actual expenditure. Do be realistic about costs; children do not come cheaply. Your list should include:

- housing costs
- utility bills
- food
- clothes
- school fees, or extra educational tuition where needed
- out-of-school activities and associated expenses
- transport
- school necessities
- electronic equipment
- sports equipment
- outings
- pocket money
- birthday parties and presents
- household necessities
- any medical expenses not covered by the National Health Service
- holidays
- hair cuts and other personal expenditure
- any special needs
- childcare if the resident parent is working
- babysitting to allow the resident parent to have a social life.

Costs of visiting

The costs of visiting a non-resident parent can be high; consider how you will divide these costs.

Change in circumstances

Earnings can increase and decrease, as can financial responsibilities if either of you acquire a new partner and have more children. The resident parent may decide to find work when the children are older. Consider what you might do if either of your situations changes in the future.

Frequency and method of payments

Once you have decided on the amount of child maintenance, you must decide how and when it is to be paid. It is important that the resident parent knows the exact date on which it will be paid. It should preferably be paid regularly, and directly, into the resident parent's bank account.

Some non-resident parents have provided a credit card for the resident parent to use for irregular large expenses, and take responsibility for making the repayments. This requires trust that the resident parent will not use the credit card for anything other than children's needs.

If the non-resident parent has sufficient assets, it may be feasible for a lump sum to be invested to cover future maintenance payments. This prevents any problems over payment if the non-resident parent's income falls, or he or she dies while the children still need to be maintained.

It may also be possible to secure the maintenance payments against an asset of the non-resident parent to provide for the children's needs if the non-resident parent's income were to fall. A life insurance policy could be taken out to cover children's needs if a non-resident parent were to die.

Review of agreements

You need to consider when your agreement should be reviewed or ended.

Enforceability of children's maintenance agreements

Once the financial agreement has been confirmed as a consent order by the court, it becomes enforceable by your former partner as a court order if you fail to make the agreed payments (see Chapter 6). Your former partner can also ask the Child Support Agency to assess your liability for maintenance. To avoid such action, discuss the matter with your former partner if you have problems in paying. It may be possible to agree to lower the payments until your financial situation improves.

Financial support and the Child Support Agency

If you and your partner fail to agree your children's financial support, you have little choice other than to apply to the Child Support Agency (CSA) for it to make a child maintenance arrangement for you. The Agency administers the scheme, introduced by the government in 1993, to force non-resident parents to maintain their children. You may be reluctant to take this route because of the Agency's reputation. One family lawyer has rather wryly warned that,

> Anyone who has done even as little as to brush up against child support law will have run away with the overwhelming sense that it is a perilous labyrinth liable quickly to enclose the unwary traveller in its clutches, never to emerge, or certainly not with anything approaching a clear appreciation of the content, direction or purpose of the subject matter.

You may agree with these comments once you have read the next section.

The scheme is now in a state of transition, and the final changes are not expected to be in place before 2013. More detailed information is available from the Child Support Agency (see 'Useful addresses' for further details).

Eligibility to apply

You can apply for an assessment to pay or receive maintenance for your children if you meet the following conditions:

- You are the children's parent. Step-parents may apply to receive maintenance for step-children living with them but cannot be assessed to pay maintenance for their step-children.
- The resident parent and children must live here.
- The non-resident parent must live here, or work abroad for the UK government or for a UK-based company.
- Your children must be under the age of 16, or under the age of 19 and in full-time education.
- Your children must not be married or have a civil partner.

How is the level of maintenance assessed?

The CSA applies one of four rates of maintenance based on the non-resident parent's income. Any income over £2,000 per week will be ignored. Any income of the resident parent is also ignored, but if they have assets over £65,000 the non-resident parent's assessment may be reduced. In 2009, the four rates were:

- *Basic rate*: non-resident parents with a net weekly income of £200 or more pay 15 per cent of it for one child, 20 per cent for two children, and 25 per cent for three or more children.
- *Reduced rate*: non-resident parents with a net weekly income of more than £100 but less than £200 a week pay £5 plus 25 per cent of any income over £100 for one child, £5 plus 35 per cent of any income over £100 for two children, £5 plus 45 per cent of any income over £100 for three or more children.
- *Flat rate*: non-resident parents with a net weekly income of £5 to £100 a week, or receiving certain state benefits, pay a flat rate of £5 per week, regardless of the number of children.
- *Nil rate*: non-resident parents with income of less than £5 a week pay nothing.

More than one family

Where a non-resident parent has children living with different resident parents, the Child Support Agency will assess the total liability and divide it equally among all the children.

Effect of state benefits

If the resident parent, or his or her new partner, is claiming state benefits, these will be reduced if the child maintenance paid to them exceeds £20 per week.

Additional factors affecting the assessment

The Child Support Agency can take into account other circumstances of a non-resident parent which may alter the level of maintenance payable. These include:

- Your children stay with you for at least 52 nights per year.
- You have other children living with you.
- You are making payments for your children under a court order.
- You have travelling costs for contact with your children.
- You have extra costs for children with disabilities living with you.
- You are repaying a debt taken on for your family's benefit before your relationship ended.
- You are paying boarding-school fees (only the boarding element may be taken into account).
- You are making payments on a loan for the former family home in which the resident parent now lives and in which you have no rights.
- You control the amount you receive in income and have deliberately reduced it by diverting it to another person for some other purpose.
- Your lifestyle suggests that you have access to assets or receive a higher income than you have declared.

The non-resident parent refuses to give information or is missing

If the non-resident parent refuses to give the necessary information, a fine can be imposed, and an order will be made of:

- £30 a week for one child
- £40 a week for two children
- £50 a week for three or more children.

If you and the Agency are unable to locate the non-resident parent, you may have to rely on state benefits if you are eligible.

Appeals

If you or your former partner disagree with the Agency's assessment, you have a right to ask for it to be reviewed. If you are still dissatisfied, you may appeal.

How payments are made

The non-resident parent may make payments directly to the resident parent or to the Child Support Agency, who will pay them to the resident parent. The Agency can also order the payments to be deducted from the non-resident parent's earnings or state benefits.

Late or missed payments

Unless the non-resident parent contacts the Child Support Agency with a good reason for defaulting on payments, the Agency will order payments to be deducted from earnings or state benefits, or it will take the parent to court. The non-resident parent may have to pay costs or have his or her driving licence confiscated, or may be sent to prison for contempt of court. The non-resident parent remains liable for the arrears.

Court orders for financial support

Most resident parents now receive financial support for their children through private agreements confirmed in a consent order, or through the Child Support Agency. However, there are a few remaining situations where parents may still be allowed to apply to court for a financial order for their children.

A consent order is in existence

If you and your former partner have made an agreement and had it confirmed as a consent order, either of you may ask the court to vary the payments.

Step-parents and a child of the family

A resident parent may apply for an order against a non-resident step-parent who has treated a child as a child of his or her family.

The non-resident parent lives abroad

If the non-resident parent lives abroad, a resident parent can apply to the court here.

Topping-up orders

If the non-resident parent earns more than £2,000 per week and the Child Support Agency has assessed maintenance up to that level, a resident parent can apply to the court for an order for additional payments to be made.

Orders for education

A resident parent can ask the court for an order for educational expenses for children under the age of 18, or for children over the age of 18 in a degree programme.

Children aged between 16 and 18

The resident parent may apply to the court for an order for children who are between 16 and 18 and not in full-time education.

Disabled children

A resident parent may apply for an order for a disabled child, regardless of whether the Child Support Agency has assessed maintenance. The order can only be for expenses connected with your child's disability.

Children's applications

Any of your children over the age of 18 may apply to the court themselves if they can show special reasons to do so. Such reasons might include education and training for a future career.

Orders against resident parents

If you are a non-resident parent you may apply to the court for an order for the resident parent to make a contribution towards the maintenance of your children when they visit you.

How the court decides financial orders

The court will consider all the circumstances, and in particular:

- the children's financial needs and resources;
- both parents' financial needs, obligations and resources;
- any physical or mental disabilities of the children;
- the standard of living enjoyed by you all before your relationship ended;
- how your children were being educated or your expectations about how they would be educated.

If you are a step-parent, the court will consider whether you took responsibility for the child's maintenance during the relationship knowing that the child was not yours, and whether there is any other person who has a duty to maintain the child.

Inheritance

You must make a will if you want your children to inherit your assets. Children may not inherit before they reach the age of 18. It is possible to set up a trust with trustees to administer your estate until then, or later if you feel that 18 is too young an age for children to manage their own affairs. You need to consult a lawyer who specializes in inheritance matters.

If you do not make a will and you remarry or become a new civil partner, any new partner will receive the first £250,000 of your assets and an interest for life in half of what remains. Your children will only inherit if there is anything left over. It can cause huge resentment if all or a large part of your assets go by default to your new partner and not to your children.

Minimize the damage to your children

Be aware of their feelings

Your children may cry, be angry, be difficult, silent or withdrawn when they realize that their parents are splitting up. Put yourself in their shoes and imagine how you might have felt at a similar age. Try to keep their concerns uppermost in your mind.

At first, your children are unlikely to take in what you say; they may be too shocked or sad even if they already felt that something was wrong. You may have had difficulty in absorbing the reality of the situation; do not expect more of your children than you do of yourself. You may have to repeat what you have told them many times over, and prepare yourself for their questions for some time to come. Try to answer honestly and accept that they might be angry with both parents.

All this may be a counsel of perfection when your world is falling apart and you can barely deal with your own emotional turmoil and worries about the practicalities facing you. However, if you are able to address your children's anxieties sensitively, in as positive a way as possible and preferably in cooperation with your partner, it may help to lessen their pain.

Adult children

Parents can be tempted to believe that what has happened will have little effect on adult children, and make the error of confiding in them and relying on them for emotional support. They may give them inappropriate information about the relationship and its failings, in the hope of getting them to take sides. This can be very damaging to family relationships, and can even lead to adult children losing confidence in their own ability to have a successful relationship.

Talk to your children

It is important for you and your partner to talk to your children about what is happening, preferably together and before their life changes dramatically. If you make no attempt to explain the situation to them, many children, even quite young ones, will use their imagination and construct their own version of reality. It is not unusual for children to feel that they are responsible. They often find it difficult to understand why, if both their parents love them and they love both their parents, they cannot stay together. They may hope that their parents will get back together and try to manipulate events to make it happen. Be honest with them and don't encourage them to think that this might happen.

When considering the time to talk to your children, choose it carefully. Discuss with your partner in advance what to tell them. Give all your attention to the children, and try not to argue with your partner or make accusations when you explain to them what is happening.

What to tell them

Clearly, what to tell your children depends on their age and maturity. Taking these into account, try to explain to them that you and their other parent will be living apart and there will be changes in their life.

With young children, it may help to draw pictures of where they will be living and with which parent. You may find that their play will reflect their reaction to what is happening. This will give you the opportunity to reassure them.

Living arrangements

If you know where and with whom they will live, tell them. If you do not know, explain that you are trying to make plans and will let them know as soon as possible. Reassure them about keeping in touch with their friends, and what will happen to their toys, clothes, pets and other possessions. If you are going to have to economize significantly, explain this to your children and ask them for their suggestions.

Their non-resident parent

It is often not practical for children to share their time equally between both their parents' homes, unless they are old enough to be independent and both parents live near each other. The majority of children are likely to live primarily with one parent. If this is so, it is important to emphasize to them that their other parent also loves and cares about them.

If it is true, tell your children that they will continue to have regular contact with both their parents and explain to them how that will work. In rare cases, because of child abuse, domestic violence or relocation abroad, it will be difficult, if not impossible, for your children to visit their non-resident parent. Explain this to them; they need to know. It is unfair to give children hope that contact will happen if it will not. If you fail to tell them the truth, they may cease to trust you.

Their family and friends

Talk to them about the other members of their family and what will happen to them. If they are not going to be living with them, explain when they will see their brothers and sisters. Will they be able to see a step-parent or other adult who has played a significant role in their life? What about grandparents, uncles, aunts and cousins – will they continue to see them? How will they be able to remain in contact with friends?

Managing change

Avoid dramatic scenes

Do your utmost to keep your discussions and emotional outbursts away from your children. Children do not need to witness them, or the final departure of a parent from the family home.

Cooperation

You may need to cooperate more with your former partner now than you did during your relationship. You will need to communicate with each other about visiting arrangements, school events, sports fixtures, medical treatment and holidays. Some super-organized parents have solved the problem by having a children's electronic diary which they can all access online. All important events are entered into it. If you feel that this is too much for you, find some alternative means of letting each other know about important events well in advance.

New homes

If possible, the resident parent should try to stay with the children in the family home. At a time of trauma, children need stability. This may, of course be impossible for financial or work reasons, or because you need to move close to family who will give you the support you need.

If the children have to move to a new home, think carefully about where it will be. Living at opposite ends of the country will not help them to adapt to their new life, and will make visits to the non-resident parent difficult and expensive.

Children should be taken to see their new home and that of the non-resident parent as soon as possible, and preferably before they move in or visit for the first time. Involve them in the process of arranging their own space in both homes, and show them around the neighbourhood.

Moving between parents

Moving between parents can be unsettling for children. It can help if they have telephone or electronic contact with their non-resident parent between visits. It will also help the non-resident parent to feel that he or she is still an important part of the children's life. Make sure that your children know how to get in touch with their non-resident parent, and try to help them to do so. Once they are old enough, let them have a mobile phone specifically for that purpose. Children can feel much more secure if they know that they can always get in touch with their non-resident parent whenever they feel the need. Non-resident parents also like to speak to their children without having to go through the resident parent first.

Encourage children to text, email and use other forms of electronic communication. Often brief regular messages from a non-resident parent can help a child who is finding separation particularly hard. Children may also want to let a non-resident parent know immediately of the triumphs of the day rather than waiting until their next visit.

Remind children of important days in their other parent's life, and encourage them to give presents and send cards.

Prepare your children for their visits to their non-resident parent. Make sure young children take their snuggly blankets, soft toys or other important items which will make them feel secure on their visits. Children will eventually have important items in both homes and may not always feel the need to move them backwards and forwards.

No matter how miserable either of you may feel when the children are with the other parent, try not to show it. Be positive about their leaving and about their return. Listen with enthusiasm to their accounts of how they spent their time, and do not run down the other parent.

Keep to arrangements and try not to change them at the last minute except for very good reasons. Always explain to each other and the children the reasons for the change.

Constant telephone calls to your children when they are visiting the non-resident parent can be damaging. Let your children make some of the decisions about when they need contact with you. If you have a good relationship with your former partner, he or she will make sure that you are contacted if it is really necessary.

Don't be persuaded by your children that their out-of-school activities or social life are always more important than visiting their non-resident parent. Involve him or her in how to resolve any difficulties.

Do not try to micro-manage the time spent with the other parent. If one parent has a slightly more liberal regime than the other, it probably does not matter. What the children do in their other parent's home is not for you to decide unless it is seriously damaging to them.

Treats are important but do not overdo them during visits, or even on return from visits. It is unfair to try to win your children's affection by spoiling them or giving them too much extra pocket money.

Your children are not messengers

Do not make your children into messengers for you and your former partner. If you need to communicate, do so yourself; it is not fair to expect your children to do it for you. Apart from anything else, children can forget to give messages. If it is hard to talk face to face, telephone, email or write a letter.

Schools

If possible, try to move children to their new school at the beginning of a new school year or new term; it will be less disruptive for them. Let your children visit the school before they begin there, and ask the school to introduce them to children who are already there. Discuss with the school what topics your children might have missed from the curriculum because of the change and how the problem can be addressed.

If your children have been through a particularly traumatic time, you need to decide what to tell their school. Be careful: if you tell too much your children may be labelled as potentially problematic, and the label becomes self-fulfilling. On the other hand, telling a school too little may lead to your children being accused of disruptive and difficult behaviour when all they need is understanding. Schools do need to know whether both parents are involved in the children's lives, and who may collect them from school if the children are too young to leave alone.

New partners

If you have a new partner, explain to your children that you have a new relationship. Take it slowly; give your children time to readjust and gradually realize that your new partner is an important part of your life. Children may find the idea of a new partner particularly difficult if their other parent does not have one; they may show resentment of yours.

If possible, do not make children meet or live with a new step-parent, or potential step-parent, immediately. Apart from your children's needs, you should be aware that children can try to sabotage new relationships, and it may require an enormous amount of patience and maturity to prevent this from happening.

You should be particularly sensitive towards your children if you were married to their other parent and your new partner is of the same sex as you.

Discuss with your new partner his or her role in your children's lives and, if he or she has children, yours in their lives. Lay down guidelines for yourselves and for your children about house rules.

Remember that your children may not like your new partner or his or her children, and may be jealous of having to share you not only with a new adult but also with new siblings. They may even worry that they will become an insignificant part of your life. Try to spend time with them on their own, when you can devote your attention solely to them.

Try not to sabotage your former partner's new relationship by preventing him or her from seeing the children on the grounds that the new relationship is damaging to them. Be honest with yourself: are you concerned that this may be a temporary relationship and you do not want your children to have a string of new quasi-step-parents, or are you jealous and simply trying to punish your partner?

Support systems

Your children will need support systems; sometimes a supportive adult, whom your children trust, may be able to talk with them and listen to their concerns in confidence. If they continue to show signs of distress, they may need more professional help (see 'Useful addresses' for information).

Safeguard their memories

Children will often have happy memories of life before your relationship ended, and these should be safeguarded. Photos can help. Even if you find them distressing, let children have photos to look at and display.

7

Your final hurdle: the legal process

Your final hurdle

Your final hurdle is to go through the legal process which will formally end your relationship. There will be forms to complete, statements to sign and swear, and a strange legal language to master. You will be aware of a relentless to-ing and fro-ing of documents between you, your partner, the court and your lawyers, if either of you has decided to engage one. You will long for the process to be over. Try not to despair or allow the process to totally dominate your life; the end really is in sight.

The special procedure

For most couples, the legal process to end their relationship will be an administrative one, known as 'the special procedure'. Unless the respondent decides to defend the petition, you will not go near a court of law. All your communication with the court will be at arm's length. If all goes smoothly, you should be able to complete the process within four to six months from the date your petition is sent to court.

If you cannot reach agreement about your property and financial affairs (see Chapter 5) or the arrangements for your children (see Chapter 6), you will have to meet with a judge, and there may ultimately be a full court hearing. In these circumstances, it is difficult to estimate how long the legal process will take; it will be under the court's control.

The courts and civil partnerships

Unlike spouses, who may use any of the divorce county courts or the Principal Registry of the Family Division in London, civil partners may only use one of the ten courts appointed to deal with the ending of civil partnership: Birmingham, Brighton, Bristol, Cardiff, Chester, Exeter, Leeds, Manchester, Newcastle and London (Principal Registry of the Family Division, London). Civil partnerships have only been in existence since 2005, and these ten courts have been designated to develop an expertise in dealing with the breakdown of civil partnerships, and applications for ancillary relief and arrangements for children.

The legal process

Decrees of divorce and dissolution orders

The petition

Only one partner, the petitioner, may begin proceedings for a decree of divorce if you are a spouse, or a dissolution order if you are a civil partner.

If you are the petitioner, you must complete a form, the petition, providing your name, address and occupation, and those of the respondent, as well as information about your children, including anyone treated as a child of the family. If either partner has changed his or her name since the marriage or civil partnership, you must say so.

You are also required to give details of the fact on which you are relying to prove that your relationship has irretrievably broken down. If you are relying on the adultery fact, and you may recall that only a spouse may do so, you must decide whether you wish to name the co-respondent. You do not have to do so, and the only legal reason for naming a co-respondent is to allow you to claim costs against them. Of course, you may wish to name the co-respondent to make yourself feel better, or even to exact revenge. Think carefully before doing so: it could rebound on you. The respondent might react badly and delay or refuse to agree any division of assets, or arrangements for the children. He or she might also deny the allegation (as might the co-respondent) and defend the divorce. Any of these reactions would delay the legal ending of your relationship.

Your petition will end with a prayer; this is the legal word for the formal request you make to the court to grant your decree or order. If you wish to claim costs against the respondent (and any co-respondent), ancillary relief for yourself or financial orders for your children, you must state that in your prayer. You may wish to go back to Chapter 6 to remind yourself of the limited circumstances in which you can apply to the court for financial orders for children. You may recall that if you do not state your intention to apply for ancillary relief in your prayer, you will need special permission from the court to do so if you later change your mind. Permission cannot be given if you have remarried or entered into a new civil partnership (see Chapter 5).

Statement of arrangements for children

You must complete a statement of arrangements if you have any children (including a child of the family) under the age of 16, or between 16 and 18 still in education or on a training programme.

In this statement you must provide the children's names, their ages and whether they have any special needs relating to their health or education. You must also give information about:

- where they are currently living and with whom;
- who cares for them if their resident parent is working;
- their financial maintenance;
- what contact they have with their non-resident parent;
- their schools, colleges or other place of education or training;
- whether there will be any changes in these arrangements after the divorce or dissolution of the civil partnership;
- whether you and the respondent have agreed on arrangements for their future, and if not, whether you are prepared to discuss the matter with a conciliator.

Filing the petition with the court

The petition and, where relevant, the statement of arrangements for the children must be sent to the court with a copy of your marriage or civil partnership certificate, and the court fee of £300 (in 2010). If you are receiving certain state benefits or have a low income, you may not have to pay this fee. The court officials will provide you with information and forms to complete if you think that you are eligible not to pay.

Acknowledgement of service

When the court receives your documents, it will send copies to the respondent (and a copy of the petition to any co-respondent). The respondent (and co-respondent) has eight days in which to reply to the court unless resident abroad, when the time limit will be extended. The reply is called acknowledgement of service. A respondent who decides to defend the divorce must file an answer within 28 days unless resident abroad, when the time limit will be extended.

Applying for directions for trial

Once the court receives the respondent's reply, it will send you a copy. Assuming the respondent agrees to your petition, you may ask the court to enter your petition into the special procedure list. This is called applying for directions for trial. With your application, you must include a signed statement, called an affidavit of evidence, in which you swear that everything you have said in your petition and statement of arrangements is true. You may ask an officer of the court or a lawyer to witness your oath and signature.

A judge will then look at all the documentation and decide whether to grant your petition. If the judge wants any further information, you will be contacted. You will not usually have to go to court.

If you and the respondent have agreed arrangements for your children, the judge will normally accept that they are satisfactory but may ask to meet you briefly to clarify matters.

Decree nisi or conditional order

If the judge decides to grant your decree or dissolution order, you will be sent a certificate showing that you are entitled to it, and the date and time when the judge will pronounce the first stage of the legal end of your relationship – a decree nisi for spouses, or a conditional order for civil partners. You do not need to attend court when this takes place.

After the decree nisi or conditional order has been pronounced, you and the respondent will be sent information explaining how to apply for the decree absolute, for spouses, or the final order, for civil partners. At the same time, you will be sent a document which states that the judge accepts that the arrangements for the children are satisfactory.

Decree absolute or final order

Six weeks and one day after the decree nisi or conditional order was granted, you must send your application for your decree absolute or final order to the court with a fee of £40 (in 2010). The court will make one final check of all the documents before sending you and the respondent a copy of the decree absolute, or final order.

Your legal relationship will now be over and you and the respondent will finally be free to go your separate ways, whether to life on your own, an informal cohabitation or, if you are not too intimidated by the legal process you have just been through, a new legal relationship.

A change of heart

If you have a change of heart before the decree nisi or conditional order has been granted, you can withdraw from the legal process. If you and the respondent both agree, you may also withdraw after the decree nisi or conditional order has been granted. Obviously, once the decree absolute or final order has been granted, it is too late. If you wish to have a legal relationship with your partner, you will have to remarry or enter into a new civil partnership.

Failure to apply for the decree or order

If you fail to apply for the decree absolute or final order, the respondent can apply three months after the date of the decree nisi or conditional order.

If either of you apply for the decree absolute or final order more than 12 months after the decree nisi or conditional order has been granted, you must send an explanation for the delay to the court with your application. You must also say whether you and the respondent have lived together during that time. If a child was born to one of you during that time, you must say whether the other partner is the biological parent of that child or has accepted the child as a child of the family.

Consent orders

Once you have obtained the decree nisi or conditional order, you may apply to the court for a consent order to confirm any agreement about the division of your assets or financial orders for your children. With your application you must include an information statement, signed by you and the respondent. This is called a statement of prescribed information, which gives the court a brief summary of:

- your financial and property resources
- pension arrangements
- mortgage arrangements
- living arrangements for the children
- any immediate plans for a new relationship.

A judge will examine your statement and will normally make the consent order without meeting with you and the respondent. If the judge is concerned about any matter, he or she may request a brief meeting with you both.

Although you may apply for a consent order after the decree nisi or conditional order has been granted, it cannot actually come into effect until you have obtained your decree absolute or final order, and no property or other assets can be transferred, or periodical payments made, until then.

Potential problems

If you experience any of the problems below, you should seek advice from an experienced family lawyer. In these circumstances, the legal ending of your relationship is likely to be considerably delayed, and will probably be more acrimonious than if you are able to cooperate with the respondent.

The respondent fails to reply to your petition

If the respondent (or co-respondent) does not reply to the court within eight days of receiving the petition, you can pay a fee and apply for a court bailiff to deliver the petition in person. After 29 days, if there is still no response, your petition can be heard by the court; the bailiff's delivery of the petition is evidence that the respondent (or co-respondent) has received it.

The time period will be extended if the respondent is living abroad.

The respondent is missing

Respondents can sometimes be difficult to trace, particularly if they have left the country and do not wish to be found. If the petition cannot be delivered, you will have to ask the court's permission to continue with the legal process. The court may agree to this once it is certain that all efforts have been made to trace the respondent.

The respondent decides to defend the petition

If the respondent decides to defend the petition, he or she must file an answer to the court. In Chapter 3, it was explained why it is rare for a respondent to defend a petition, and even rarer to succeed.

A respondent should ask him- or herself the reasons for wanting to defend the petition. It may give you satisfaction to have your version of the relationship heard, but little else. You will be encouraged to try to find a solution at a mediation appointment with a judge. If you are unable to do so, there will have to be a court hearing. Your relationship will almost certainly be legally ended, but at a cost.

The respondent decides to issue a cross-petition

If on receiving the petition you want to be the one who ends the relationship, you may issue a cross-petition. You will then become the cross-petitioner and the petitioner will become the cross-respondent.

The court will have to decide whose petition to grant or whether to issue cross-decrees of divorce or cross-dissolution orders.

The model Katie Price and the singer Peter Andre were one of the rare couples granted cross-decrees when they divorced each other in 2009.

You and the respondent are unable to agree about the division of assets

If you cannot agree about the division of your assets, you will be asked by the court to attend a meeting called a First Appointment. At this appointment, if you reach agreement, a judge will make a final order.

If agreement cannot be reached, an appointment will be made for a Financial Dispute Resolution Hearing, or the judge may adjourn your case to allow you to go to an independent mediator to help you reach an agreement. The court will set a timetable and you will be asked to complete a financial statement which must be sworn and sent to the court. You must both disclose all your assets. Failure to do so can result in an increase in your costs or even imprisonment for contempt of court.

If there is still no agreement, an appointment will be made for a Final Hearing before a different judge. At this meeting, the judge will consider all the information relating to your assets and make a final order.

It is possible that your ancillary relief will not be finalized until after you have obtained the decree absolute or final order. The court may also decide to delay the grant of the decree absolute or final order until the ancillary relief has been finalized.

You and the respondent cannot agree the arrangements for the children

Where you have been unable to agree the arrangements for the children, the court will arrange a Conciliation Appointment which you and the respondent and any children over the age of nine must attend. The point of this meeting is to encourage you to cooperate and make plans which you and the children find acceptable. An officer from the Children and Family Court Advisory and Support Services (CAFCASS) will also be present to help. The CAFCASS officer will speak to the children privately to try to find out what they would like to happen, and then report back to the judge.

If you are unable to agree, a Directions Appointment will be made. At this meeting, the judge will ask you and the respondent to provide a formal statement of what order you would like to have made for the children. A CAFCASS officer will be asked to visit the children and talk to you and the respondent to find out what everyone would like to happen. The CAFCASS officer may also talk with any other professionals involved with the family, such as doctors and social workers, and report their views on how the children's future should be decided to the court.

There will then be a Final Hearing and the court will make an order, unless, of course, you and the respondent have managed to agree before then.

The court will not issue a decree absolute or a final order until the arrangements for the children have been decided.

Decrees of judicial separation and separation orders

For those of you who wish to apply for a decree of judicial separation, or a separation order, the process is very similar to that for obtaining decrees of divorce or dissolution orders.

The major differences are:

- You do not need to prove that the relationship has broken down. When you complete the petition, if you are a spouse, you merely give details of one of the five facts on which you are relying to obtain the decree. If you are a civil partner, you will give details of one of the four facts on which you are relying to obtain the order.
- The grave hardship rule does not apply if you are relying on fact 5, living apart for five years (see Chapter 3).
- If the respondent agrees to the petition and the court agrees to grant the decree or order, it will be granted as a decree of judicial separation absolute or a final separation order immediately; there will be no preliminary stage of a decree nisi or a conditional order.

Arrangements for ancillary relief and children

Arrangements for ancillary relief and children after separation proceedings will be decided in the same way as in cases of divorce, or dissolution of civil partnerships.

Potential problems

The problems which are likely to arise in separation proceedings will be similar to those which happen in proceedings for divorce, or dissolution of civil partnerships, and they will be resolved in the same way.

Divorce or dissolution after the grant of a decree of judicial separation or separation order

If you decide that you wish to obtain a decree of divorce or a dissolution order after you have already obtained a separation decree or order, you may do so. However, there are no short cuts; you must petition for divorce or dissolution as described above.

Decrees of nullity and nullity orders

As we saw in Chapter 4, applications for decrees or order of nullity are not common. In spite of these very small numbers, an explanation of the legal process to obtain a decree or order of nullity is included here to complete the picture. It must be emphasized that you should consult a specialist family lawyer if you believe that you have reasons to have your relationship annulled.

The petition

Your petition for nullity will follow closely that of a petition for divorce, dissolution or separation. The main difference is that instead of pleading one of the facts, you state the ground on which you are basing your petition (see Chapter 4). You do not state that the relationship has irretrievably broken down in a petition for nullity because you are trying to prove that your relationship does not exist, that it is invalid.

Along with your petition, statement of arrangements for children, the fee and your marriage or civil partnership certificate, you must include, where relevant, your interim gender recognition certificate. The certificate must not be more than six months old.

Going to court

Once you have submitted your petition to the court, you will have to attend court, even if the respondent has sent an acknowledgement of service and does not wish to defend the petition. The court always tries to handle nullity cases with exceptional sensitivity. It will require evidence of the ground on which you have based your petition. In the case of non-consummation, medical reports for both you and the respondent may be required.

If the respondent decides to defend your petition or submit a cross-petition for nullity, he or she will also have the opportunity to be heard by the court.

Before deciding whether to grant your nullity decree or nullity order, the court will also have to decide whether it would be unjust to the respondent to do so.

If the court agrees to grant your petition, it will do so in two stages. There will first be a decree nisi or conditional order of nullity, and six weeks and one day later, you may apply for the decree absolute or final order of nullity. If you fail to apply for the decree at that time, the same rules apply as in cases of divorce or dissolution of a civil partnership.

Arrangements for ancillary relief and children

Arrangements for ancillary relief and children after nullity proceedings will be considered in the same way as in cases of divorce, dissolution of civil partnerships and separation.

Potential problems

The problems which are likely to arise in nullity proceedings will be similar to those which happen in proceedings for divorce, dissolution of civil partnerships and separation, and they will be resolved in the same way.

Engaging a lawyer

If your affairs are complex or you feel that it would be less stressful to hand over responsibility to an expert family lawyer (and perhaps a tax consultant too), you will probably feel a huge sense of relief that you are not on your own as you go through the legal process to end your relationship.

Contrary to popular rumour, family lawyers are not there to increase the conflict between you and your partner. They are there to protect you, explain matters to you, give you sound advice, deal with the bureaucracy which is characteristic of the legal process, negotiate the division of your assets, and help resolve the arrangements for your children. They will act as an intermediary between you and your partner, and should help you through the final stage in as calm a way as is possible (see 'Useful addresses' for information on how to find a family lawyer).

Prepare in advance

Before going to see a lawyer, it may be good idea to do some groundwork and try to understand the legal process. You should make a list of any matters you wish to discuss or questions you want to ask. Gather as much information as you can about your and your partner's assets. Have some idea about what you would like to achieve in terms of division of assets and arrangements for your children. Your lawyer will soon tell you whether you are being realistic. Doing the groundwork will help to centre your thoughts as well as saving you time and money.

Going it alone

The information in this chapter primarily explains the procedure to be used in situations which are straightforward. I have highlighted those circumstances where I think that you should consult a lawyer rather than go it alone. Remember that it is not generally advisable to act for yourself if your partner does not want your relationship to end, has disappeared, or is not prepared to agree the division of assets or arrangements for the children, or if you want to apply for a decree or order of nullity.

If you do decide to do the legal dismantling of your relationship yourself, be realistic about the task ahead. Although it can be an empowering process for you, as well as an economical one, it will also be time-consuming and frustrating. You will need abundant patience. Be prepared to be meticulous. You will have to obtain all the documents required for each stage of the legal process. Copies must be kept of every form you complete, every statement you swear and every letter you send or receive. It will help to have access to a computer, the internet, a printer, a scanner, a photocopier and a fax machine.

A change of mind

Do remember that, at any time, you can change your mind and seek the help of a lawyer if you feel the need to do so. It will not be an admission of defeat.

Obtaining forms

All the relevant forms and detailed information on how to complete them are available on Her Majesty's Courts Service (HMCS) website, where they can be downloaded free of charge (see 'Useful addresses' for further details). You will also find a list of courts on the website where court officials are available who can provide further information or help with completion of forms; they are not, however, allowed to give you legal advice.

Congratulate yourself

Once your decree or order has been granted and you have finalized the division of assets and arrangements for your children, you will be able to congratulate yourself on your achievement; you will deserve it.

8

Facing the future

Facing the future

Rather like the planning of a wedding or a civil partnership, the legal process of ending a relationship has a tendency to take over and dominate life. Although you may be relieved when it is finally over, you may also find that a large gap opens up. The adrenalin no longer flows. It is rather like the aftermath of running a marathon, having a baby or securing a business deal. It can be something of a let-down, even for those who have a new relationship waiting for them. Reality hits, and the question is, what now?

Take your time, treat yourself kindly, be positive and be prepared to take risks. This new phase of your life can be a valuable learning experience. You may discover new aspects of yourself, or rediscover talents and qualities which were stifled or dormant during the relationship you have left behind.

Celebrations or wakes

In America, it is not unusual to mark the end of a relationship with a celebratory party, cards and presents. For those with religious beliefs, a church service may be held.

Until recently, the more conservative British have been reluctant to follow this transatlantic approach. There are, however, signs of change. In 2009, the first 'starting over' fair was held and, rather like at a wedding fair, participants were offered a range of services, including advice on planning receptions, parties and rituals to celebrate the end of a relationship and mark the beginning of a new phase of life. Beware; in 2009, one recently divorced woman was murdered by her former partner when she put up banners outside her home announcing her divorce party to her friends.

You may question whether it is appropriate to throw a large party to celebrate the failure of a relationship which you entered with joy and optimism. However, if you feel positive and happy about your new status, you might wish to mark it, and bid farewell to the past, with a gathering of supportive friends. If you decide that you would like a religious service, talk to the appropriate person at your place of worship who may be prepared to help you.

If you are very unhappy about the ending of your relationship, some form of ritual, attended by very close friends, might also be beneficial. Rather like a funeral, it can help you to begin the process of mourning the past and allow you to move towards acceptance, and a belief that a new and happy life is perfectly possible.

For those of you who loathe the idea of any formal celebration of your new status, or mourning the loss of your former relationship, you might like give yourself a present to mark the beginning of this new phase in your life.

Whether celebrating or mourning, few will be able to follow the example of the former Mrs Bernie Ecclestone, who bought a £36.5 million jet to mark her divorce from her billionaire husband.

Emotional stocktaking

Whether you are happy and relieved or sad and depressed about the end of your relationship, you may find it worthwhile to examine why it failed. Relationships break down for many different reasons and the breakdown is rarely entirely the fault of one partner. If you are contemplating, or are already in, a new relationship, emotional stocktaking can be particularly important. You do not wish to repeat the same mistakes.

You might find it helpful to begin by considering three questions:

- Why did you begin a relationship with your former partner?
- What part do you think you played in its breakdown?
- In what way did the relationship prevent either you or your former partner from achieving your potential?

Your answers to these questions may help you gain some understanding of yourself which will help you face the future.

Therapy or counselling

You might decide to find a therapist or counsellor to help you with your emotional stocktaking. Although many people regard therapy and counselling at best as self-indulgent and at worst as useless, emotional pain may make you think differently. It can be just as difficult to bear as physical pain, and may force you into seeking professional help.

Therapy or counselling can be very beneficial when you confront a problem which seems impossible to resolve, and which you have faced many times before. So much of our behaviour in relationships is an automatic, inappropriate and often subconscious response to a partner's conduct, and not a conscious adult response to what is actually happening. You may be aware that you repeat history and behave in destructive ways which you do not understand and which you feel are everyone's fault but yours. Untangling and reaching an understanding of all this, without help, is not an easy task.

Supportive friends, no matter how well-meaning, do not like to challenge your behaviour. They want to make you feel comfortable and not distress you further. They can also feel threatened by your failed relationship; it might make them feel insecure about their own. Therapists and counsellors are tougher, albeit empathetic, creatures. They will encourage you to confront difficult questions and will not allow you to escape with easy answers.

If you decide that you would like the help of a therapist or counsellor, find one with whom you feel comfortable. Most will meet with you for a preliminary session to allow you both to decide whether you can work together.

Going it alone

If you are therapy- or counselling-phobic, or unable to afford the costs, you may have to do your emotional stocktaking alone. One exercise which can be helpful is to write your autobiography. Be honest with yourself: this is not an autobiography for publication as a best-selling blockbuster. It is for your eyes alone, to help you uncover what has affected your major decisions in life, particularly your choice of former partner.

Acknowledging reality

It is important to acknowledge the good parts as well as the bad parts of your former relationship. It is rare that a relationship is totally bad. However, many people are afraid to recognize the good aspects of it, and find it all to easy to emphasize the bad. That way they are able to justify the failure of the relationship and free themselves from any responsibility.

Guilt

Guilt can be an overwhelming emotion if you left the relationship because you fell in love with someone else, or because you wanted to follow a personal passion which had been stifled during the relationship. You need to try to find a way of dealing with guilt. If you do not, you will find that it can raise its head in the future, often when least expected, and create chaos in your new life. Sometimes a person who experiences strong feelings of guilt may even try to return to the former relationship, usually with disastrous consequences.

Acknowledging guilt to yourself, to your former partner if that seems appropriate, and to your children if they are old enough, can be helpful. You can be sorry for their pain while at the same time accepting that you had to leave the relationship for your own survival.

The Grief Cycle

For most people, the failure of a relationship and the consequent change in lifestyle is hard. Even if a relationship has been a difficult one, many partners will have had some enjoyment, comfort and stability from a home and a familiar way of life. Once the relationship is over, you may try to avoid the pain caused by the loss of the familiar. Yet, rather like mourning the death of a close family member or friend, you must eventually confront this pain to move on and feel content in your new life. The process necessary to reach this place has been described as 'the Grief Cycle', and involves five stages. Understanding the stages of the Grief Cycle can be helpful in recovering at the end of a relationship.

Denial

The first stage of the cycle is denial. Your life has been turned upside down, and nothing will ever be the same again. You may be very frightened, feel ill, paralysed and incapable of any action and would prefer to lurk under your duvet. Yet you pretend that everything is all right. You try to convince yourself and others that life has not really changed significantly. You may even secretly hope that you will get back together with your former partner.

Anger

Denial may be followed by anger when the reality of your new life finally hits home. The anger may be directed at your former partner, or even at yourself if you feel that the breakdown of the relationship was your fault.

Bargaining

You may attempt to stall the changes to your life and try to bargain your way out of the pain. In extreme cases, this can even involve attempts to revive the relationship in some way. The cost of bargaining is high and may be at the expense of your own personal development, which will only begin to happen when you accept the reality that your relationship has legally ended.

Depression

Bargaining is often followed by depression as you realize that there is no going back. You recognize that returning to a relationship is rarely a good idea, or even possible. Although depression may not feel like a good place to be, it can bring about change. If depression overwhelms you or continues for a long period of time, you may need to seek help from your doctor, or a therapist or counsellor.

Acceptance

The final stage of the Grief Cycle is acceptance, which can lead you to explore a new life for yourself.

Grief – an individual experience

You may find your own experience of the Grief Cycle not quite so straightforward. You may have experienced all five stages before the legal end of your relationship, yet still find yourself revisiting some of them when the reality of your post-relationship becomes clear. Anger and depression, in particular, are likely to raise their heads more than once.

Those of you who have not faced up to your grief before may now find yourselves in the clutches of the Grief Cycle for the first time.

It is important not to become too stuck in any one stage of the Grief Cycle. Some people find it difficult to move on from anger and actually feed it. One woman made a career for herself by giving television and radio interviews based on her obsessive anger at her husband's betrayal. She gathered a group of like-minded people around her who shared and encouraged each other in their anger.

If you are finding it difficult to move on, it might be better to keep away from a former partner if you can. For those of you with children who cannot avoid contact with a former partner, try to limit it to what is absolutely necessary.

Supporting your children

You may find it helpful to look again at Chapter 6; all the matters discussed there will be equally applicable at this stage.

Remember that once you and your former partner are living apart, children may find it even more distressing for the first year or so than when you were in the throes of leaving each other. Their dreams of their parents reuniting have been dashed and they are likely to have to face further changes to their lifestyle. You may have to be extra understanding if they continue to display emotional distress or act in an anti-social way.

Take care when dating new people. Your children do not need to meet every person you date. Be wary about bringing dates home when your children are there; it can be very confusing for them to meet a string of people whom they may view as a potential step-parent even if you do not. Never leave children alone with anyone until you are certain they present no threat to them.

If you do begin a new relationship and acquire step-children, remember that this may trigger behavioural problems for your own children as well as your step-children. Both can be very resentful about their parent's new partner. Try to discuss some ground rules with your children, your new partner and your step-children. Relying on rules can help to deflect angry refusals by step-children to obey you because you are not their parent.

Rebuilding your life

While emotional stocktaking is important, so is examining some of the more practical aspects of your life and deciding what to do about them.

Creating a new home

Moving house at the end of a relationship can be a very traumatic experience but it can also be immensely beneficial. You will be able to create a new environment which is entirely yours, and in which you feel secure and comfortable. It is a way of laying the ghosts of your past life and becoming an independent person.

If you decide, or are forced for financial reasons, to remain in the family home, transform it into your own personal space, a symbol of your new life. Your former partner has no say in this project. You do not need to be extravagant, and you may not have the resources to do so, but it is still possible to be creative.

Social life

Friends are essential. If you find that, along with the loss of your relationship, you have lost some of your friends, seize it as an opportunity to explore new friendships. They may be more appropriate for the person you have become as a result of your experiences.

Be brave about accepting invitations and trying out new activities. You may discover a new world for yourself out there, and if they do not work out, you will have lost nothing.

New relationships

Hope tends to triumph over the experience of a failed relationship. You may have found a new relationship before leaving the old one. Be aware that problems can arise in new relationships once you are free to live with each other. The reality of everyday life, and possibly the presence of step-children, is very different from the romantic excitement at the beginning of a relationship. Do not give up at this point; discuss problems when they arise rather than allowing them to grow into insurmountable ones. You do not want to have to face yet another failed relationship.

You may prefer to recuperate from the loss of your relationship before contemplating a new one. Once you are ready to do so, you may feel a little nervous, particularly if your former relationship was a long one and you have not dated for many years. Remember that many of the people whom you are likely to meet will have similar fears to yours.

While you may hope to meet a new partner in the normal course of everyday life, you might be more successful if you widen your search. If you can afford it, a good introduction agency is probably your best option. Do your research and choose carefully. Any worthwhile agency will take a professional approach to its clients. It will interview all of them personally and in depth. It will take the matter of confidentiality seriously. You should also interview the agency to ensure that, provided that you are being realistic, your expectations match. Ask about its client base and its success rates, particularly if you are an older client.

Decide whether its clients are the sorts of people you would like to meet. A reputable agency should be prepared to be honest with you and will not take you on if it believes it cannot help you. It should also be prepared to hold your hand a little and give you some general advice if you have not dated for a long time. All dates should be followed up by the agency, and you should always be given feedback soon after the date.

Other riskier, although increasingly popular, ways of finding a new partner, if you cannot afford an agency, are online dating sites, or newspaper and magazine dating columns.

Whatever route you choose, do be cautious. You can be emotionally vulnerable when emerging from a relationship and may be susceptible to the advances of the first person who shows a romantic interest in you, regardless of his or her suitability.

When meeting someone for the first time, make sure that you have a mobile phone with you and always meet in a public place. Let one or two friends know when and where you are going, with whom, and when you expect to return. Phone them on your return to let them know that you are safe. Do not arrange to invite anyone home or accept invitations to their homes, or hotel rooms, until you know them sufficiently well to feel safe.

Discussion about contraception and the avoidance of sexually transmitted diseases is always a good idea before beginning a new sexual relationship. These are important matters, and it is not worth taking sexual risks with anyone who is not prepared to discuss them or who shows a lack of interest in them. It demonstrates their lack of concern for you.

Do not rush into living with a new partner; give yourselves time to enjoy the fun of a new relationship, and decide whether it has the potential to be satisfying in the long term.

Employment or retraining

Many people use the end of a relationship as an opportunity to change career direction if financial demands permit. Take time to explore the possibilities open to you, and try not to be too rigid in your approach. Balance a realistic assessment of your capabilities with an openness to acquiring new skills.

This may be the time to retrain or go into higher education. Many institutions welcome older students and provide flexible programmes which would allow you to work part-time while studying. Make appointments to talk to admissions tutors, ask about scholarships and bursaries, and be prepared to consider loans. The long-term benefits of education or training may outweigh the short-term financial gains of employment now.

If you have to face working for the first time in many years, you may find yourself having to balance work and childcare. Take time to make sure that you have put in place arrangements which work. There is nothing worse than returning to work and having to take time out because your childcare breaks down.

Financial and administrative matters

Budgets

Unless you are fortunate, you will probably have to budget carefully to survive financially. Be positive; this is your budget and not under your former partner's control. You can decide for yourself what is important to you and what you might be prepared to sacrifice.

If you have a computer, use a standard spreadsheet on which to list all your income and expenditure. Once the figures are in front of you, it is much easier to decide where you can make cuts, or how much extra income you need to make. You may have to do this for several months to get a good picture of your financial situation. It can be very satisfying to realize that you can afford to live within your income.

Make sure that you are applying for all state benefits and tax relief to which you are entitled.

Try to build into your budget provision for treats and a social life. If you have children, include an allowance for babysitters; you need to have a break from your children and enjoy adult company from time to time.

Potential financial problems

Past debts

If you have not already done so, you should now make sure that you let your bank, credit card companies and any other lenders know that your former relationship has legally ended, and that you wish to freeze or close all joint accounts. Any debt which you incurred jointly with your former partner will generally remain the responsibility of both of you. However, you want to ensure that no further debts are incurred on any joint accounts.

Payments from your former partner

If your former partner defaults on ongoing payments for you or your children, or on mortgage payments, take action immediately; do not wait for debts to mount up. If possible, talk to your former partner about the problem and find out whether it is a short-term difficulty which you can weather. If it is not, you may need to seek legal help to enforce payments (see Chapter 5). You may also need to apply for social security benefits, or make an application to the Child Support Agency (see Chapter 6).

Bank overdrafts and loans

If you do have a temporary shortfall in income, talk to your bank. Unauthorized overdrafts are very expensive; if possible ask your bank to authorize one or agree a loan.

Credit and store card debts

Do not be tempted to run up debts on credit or store cards; interest rates will be very high. Rather, use these cards as a convenient method of managing your budget and try to pay them off every month.

Change passwords

Remember to change passwords and PINs on accounts which you have shared with your former partner.

Wills

If you have not already done so, remember to make a will to reflect your new circumstances. If you have a new partner and children from your previous relationship, you may want to consider how to divide your property in a way which will give your children a fair share. If you do not make a will, any new legal partner will automatically inherit a share of your estate, and your children may lose out (see Chapter 5 for further details).

Administrative matters

Documentation

This may be a good opportunity to sort out all your personal documents and start a new file in which to keep copies of all your important personal documents, beginning with the decree or order which ended your relationship and your new will. You should include copies of your and your children's birth certificates; your marriage or civil partnership certificates; your and your children's passports, insurance documents, and pension and other financial information. You will probably want to add to this list.

Who to inform about your new legal status

If you have not already done so, make a list of all those who need to be informed about your new legal status and contact details. They may require proof of your status so make sure that you have plenty of copies of the relevant documents. The list below should help you with this rather tedious task. You may need to modify it to meet your own circumstances:

- mortgage lender
- landlord
- housing benefit office
- council tax office
- water, gas, electricity and telephone companies
- social security office
- tax office
- your children's present school and their future school if they are about to start a new school
- bank and credit card companies
- hire purchase or credit companies
- insurance companies
- the Post Office, for redirection of your mail
- doctor, dentist and any other health providers
- TV Licensing
- the Driver and Vehicle Licensing Agency (DVLA) for changes to driving licence and vehicle registration details
- lawyers and executors.

Do not forget to give your new details to all those family members and friends with whom you wish to remain in contact.

Your life is in your hands

When a relationship ends, it can be tempting to lay the blame on others when life becomes uncomfortable. If you are alone, your former partner may become the target of your blame. If you are in a new relationship, you may blame your new partner. Try to avoid doing this. Take responsibility for your new life and control of your own future.

Develop self-reliance

Self-reliance is an important quality whether you are in a relationship or not; cultivate it. Remind yourself that you have resources of your own which have perhaps been hidden up to now; this is your chance to develop them. However, do not be afraid to ask for help when necessary.

A potentially exciting journey

More than anything else, remind yourself that this new phase of life is a potentially exciting journey on which you have embarked. Arriving at a destination is not important; learning how to live contentedly en route is. For some of you, this may be a sad part of the journey, but you will gradually become happier and gain in confidence as you distance yourself from the breakdown of your relationship.

Glossary

acknowledgement of service The document the court sends with the petition to end the relationship to the respondent. It must be completed and returned to the court.

affidavit of evidence The statement signed and sworn by the petitioner to confirm that all the facts in the petition and the statement of arrangements for children are true.

ancillary relief The redistribution of property and other assets after the legal end of a relationship.

annulment A decree or order of nullity.

application for directions for trial The petitioner's request to court to be entered into the 'special procedure' list for the decree of divorce or judicial separation, or dissolution or separation order, to be granted.

attachment of earnings A court order for money to be taken directly from earnings to pay a debt.

Children and Family Court Advisory and Support Services (CAFCASS) CAFCASS takes care of children's interests in family legal proceedings. It advises the court on what it considers to be in the best interests of the children.

Central Attachment of Earnings Payment System (CAPS) CAPS takes care of all attachment of earnings orders (except those issued by the magistrates' courts). It monitors and processes orders for payment and, where enforcement is required, refers orders back to the court.

child abduction A parent's removal or retention of a child without the other parent's consent or a court order.

Child Maintenance and Enforcement Commission (CMEC) A new Non-Departmental Public Body responsible for the child maintenance system in the UK. The Child Support Agency will continue to operate under it, in a period of transition, until 2013.

child of the family A child, other than a foster child, who has been treated by a person as a child of his or her family.

Child Support Agency (CSA) The CSA is now part of the Child Maintenance and Enforcement Commission. Its role is to make sure that non-resident parents contribute financially to their children's upkeep when parents have been unable to agree an arrangement themselves. It is in a state of transition expected to last until 2013.

civil partnership   The Civil Partnership Act 2004 came into force in 2005. It allows same-sex couples to register a civil partnership and obtain almost all the rights and responsibilities of married couples. Opposite sex couples may not become civil partners.

clean break order   A court order after the legal end of a relationship which ends any further property and financial, and usually inheritance, claims by one partner against the other. It does not end claims for children.

co-respondent   The person with whom the respondent is alleged to have committed adultery.

cohabitant   A person who lives in an opposite-sex or same-sex relationship without marrying or registering a civil partnership. Cohabitants have very limited rights when they part.

collaborative law   A four-way process in which both partners and their lawyers conduct negotiations face to face. Its aim is to resolve disputes without going to court. If negotiations fail, the couple must choose new lawyers.

conciliation   The process in which a couple meets with a neutral mediator to try to reach an agreement about children and property and financial disputes.

Conciliation Appointment   An informal court hearing held in private, after you have been unable to reach an agreement with your partner about arrangements for your children. Both partners, their lawyers, the judge and sometimes a CAFCASS officer will be present. Children may be asked to attend.

conditional order   The first stage of the two-part process to end a civil partnership by dissolution or annulment.

consent order   A court order which confirms an agreement between partners about their property and financial assets or maintenance agreements for children. The order can be enforced or varied in the same way as any other court order.

contact order   A court order for parental contact with his or her children. Direct contact can be for any period of time which the court believes appropriate. Orders can be made for supervised contact, or indirect contact in the form of letters, emails or telephone communication.

cross-petition   A petition issued by a respondent who wants a divorce but on the basis of his or her petition rather than the petitioner's. The court may grant the decree or order on the basis of the petition or the cross-petition, or as a cross-decree or order.

decree absolute   The final court order which legally ends a marriage.

decree nisi   The first stage of divorce or annulment of a marriage.

decree of nullity   The court order in proceedings for annulment.

defending the petition   The response to the petition by a partner who objects to the petition and does not want the relationship to be legally ended.

Directions Appointment   The first court hearing to consider ancillary relief when the partners have been unable to reach an agreement.

dissolution order   The order which ends a civil partnership.

domicile   The country you regard as home, whether or not you live there. You may retain a domicile in another country because you hope to return there.

earmarking   A means of ordering a pension to be paid to a non-pension-owning partner at the date of retirement of the pension-owning partner.

estate   The assets owned at the time of death and available for distribution under the will, or by law if there is no will.

family home   Any property lived in by a couple and their children. There can be more than one family home and it can be a caravan or boat or perhaps a tent.

filing an answer   The defence to a petition made by a respondent who is opposed to the grant of a decree or order.

filing the petition   The submission of the petition to the court.

Final Hearing   The last stage of the court proceedings in ancillary relief disputes.

final order   The last stage of the legal ending of a civil partnership.

Financial Dispute Resolution Hearing   The second stage of the court proceedings in ancillary relief disputes.

First Appointment   The first stage of the court proceedings in ancillary relief disputes.

habitual residence The place in which you normally live.

Her Majesty's Court Service (HMCS) An executive agency of the Ministry of Justice; it manages the courts and gives information to the public about legal procedures. Its website offers a wide range of information. Forms can be downloaded without charge.

housing benefit A benefit for people on a low income and with little capital to help them pay their rent. It does not cover mortgage or home loans. They may be covered by state benefits.

interim gender recognition certificate The Gender Recognition Act 2004 allows those who change sex after marriage or a civil partnership to apply to a Gender Recognition Panel for an interim gender recognition certificate. The certificate permits an application for an annulment of the relationship.

interim maintenance Court-ordered payments to partners before the final order for ancillary relief.

joint tenants Each partner has an equal interest in the property and in the proceeds of sale, regardless of contribution to the purchase price of, or expenditure on, the property. If one partner dies, the whole of the property will belong to the surviving partner regardless of anything in the will to the contrary.

judicial separation The legal process which allows spouses to live apart, apply for ancillary relief but not remarry or enter into a civil partnership. They retain the status of spouse.

Land Registry It keeps the register of title to registered land in England and Wales and records all dealings with it. The register is accessible to the public.

legal aid The Legal Services Commission (LSC) is responsible for financing help for access to legal advice, information and help. Specific enquires for legal aid are dealt with by the Community Legal Advice helpline (see 'Useful addresses').

lump sum orders Ancillary relief orders for a transfer of capital in cash.

maintenance Ancillary relief orders to financially support a former partner; they may be made by payment of a lump sum or by periodical payments.

marriage or civil partnership settlements A fund set up to provide for the needs of a spouse or civil partner or children during or after the relationship has ended, usually administered by trustees on a discretionary basis, Settlements may have tax advantages.

mediation The process in which a couple meet with a neutral mediator to try to reach an agreement about children and property and financial disputes.

non-resident parent The parent with whom the child does not live on a regular basis but who plays a role in the child's life.

occupation order A short-term court order which permits a partner to occupy, or re-enter, the family home against the other partner's wishes. They are often used in cases of domestic violence.

order of nullity The order granted to a civil partner after annulment proceedings.

parental alienation syndrome The resident parent's efforts to disparage the non-resident parent and brainwash their child into refusing contact with the non-resident parent.

parental responsibility All the legal rights, duties, powers and responsibilities a parent has in relation to a child and his or her property.

periodical payments Regular payments under a court order for ancillary relief; they may be for maintenance or as compensation for contribution to the relationship.

perjury Lying about matters which you have sworn on oath to be true.

petition The document which the partner who begins the legal process to end the relationship (the petitioner) submits to the court.

prayer This is the final part of the petition; the petitioner asks the court to grant the decree or order and, if he or she wants to apply for ancillary relief and/or costs, a statement to that effect.

prohibitive steps order A court order forbidding a person from carrying out a specific act in relationship to a child.

reconciliation The decision of partners to stay together rather than to legally end their relationship.

residence order A court order for a child to live with a specific person.

resident parent The parent with whom the child lives for the majority of the time.

Resolution   Formerly the Solicitors' Family Law Association; its members are family lawyers committed to a non-confrontational approach and considering the needs of all the family, particularly the best interests of the children.

right to occupy the family home   Any partner who does not have a legal right in the family home may register a right to occupy the home at the Land Registry against the title of the partner with the legal right. A right of occupation, if registered, can be exercised even if the property changes hands.

secured periodical payments   Regular payments made by one partner to the other and secured against property, or another asset, which can be sold in case of default on payments, or on the death of the partner making the payments.

separation order   The equivalent of a decree of spousal judicial separation for civil partners, it allows them to live apart and apply for ancillary relief. They retain the status of civil partner and may not marry or enter into a new civil partnership.

severing the joint tenancy   A means of changing the way you own property into a tenancy in common. It enables you to share in the proceeds of sale unequally, and to leave your share wish by will. If you sever, you should notify the Land Registry.

shared residence   The children alternate living between the homes of both parents.

specific issue order   An order relating to a specific aspect of a child's life.

state benefits   A wide range of means-tested and non-means-tested state payments, to ensure basic living requirements are met.

statement of arrangements for children   The form which a petitioner completes giving information about the children of the family and any plans agreed for their future.

statutory charge   The debt owed if you have claimed legal aid for ancillary relief, and you were awarded property or allowed to retain property. The charge will be secured against the property.

step-child   A child who lives with the partner of his or her biological or adoptive parent or parent who has obtained parental rights after infertility treatment in a licensed clinic or after surrogacy.

step-parent   A married or civil partner who lives with the children of a partner.

tenancy in common   Each partner has a specified share of the property, normally recorded in a legal document. On sale the proceeds are divided according to the specified share. On death the deceased's share is inherited according to the will or, if there is no will, by the beneficiaries specified in law.

topping-up order   A court order for child support where the CSA has assessed a non-resident parent's liability up to the maximum level permitted (currently £2,000 net per week).

wardship   The High Court can make children wards of court where they have been abducted or are in serious danger or at risk. The court takes responsibility for them, and no action which affects the children can be taken by any person without the court's permission.

Useful addresses

1 My relationship is in difficulties

General information on relationships and relationship counselling

British Association for Counselling & Psychotherapy (BACP)
Tel.: 01455 883300
www.bacp.co.uk

Counselling Directory
www.counselling-directory.org.uk
A comprehensive online database of UK counsellors and psychotherapists containing information on training, experience and fees.

Couples Counselling Network
www.ukcouplescounselling.com
A website providing details of counsellors who specialize in counselling couples in difficulties with their relationship, either face to face or online.

Relate
Tel.: 0300 100 1234
www.relate.org.uk

Samaritans
Tel. 08457 90 90 90
www.samaritans.org
Provide confidential emotional support 24 hours a day every day of the year to those experiencing despair, distress or suicidal feelings.

The United Kingdom Council for Psychotherapy (UKCP)
Tel.: 020 7014 9955
www.psychotherapy.org.uk

2 The end has come: what now?

Collaborative law

Collaborative Family Lawyers
www.collaborativefamilylawyers.co.uk
Trained professional lawyers who work through a system of Collaborative Practice to help resolve disputes without going to court. Further details, including locations, are available via the website.

Domestic violence

The Home Office
www.homeoffice.gov.uk
Provides general information on domestic violence and the site contains related links. See also <www.crimereduction.homeoffice.gov.uk>.

Men's Advice Line Helpline
Tel.: 020 8644 9914

National Centre for Domestic Violence
Tel.: 0844 8044 999
Freephone service accessed by first phoning 080009 70 20 70
www.ncdv.org.uk

National Domestic Violence Helpline
Tel.: 0808 2000 247 (free, 24 hours every day)
www.nationaldomesticviolencehelpline.org.uk
Run in partnership with **Refuge** and **Women's Aid** (see below). Provides a free fast emergency service to survivors of domestic violence regardless of gender, race, sexual orientation or financial circumstances.

Refuge
Tel.: 020 7395 7700 (general admin matters)
http://refuge.org.uk
Set up the world's first refuge for women and children escaping domestic violence nearly 40 years ago. Now helps over 900 women and children every day. A partner in running the National Domestic Violence Helpline.

Women's Aid
Tel.: 0117 944 4411 (general admin matters)
www.womensaid.org.uk
Gives details through a domestic-abuse directory of where help can be obtained in your area. A partner in running the National Domestic Violence Helpline.

Finding a lawyer

Lawyer Locator
Tel.: 020 8662 2058 (enquiries: 9 a.m. to 5 p.m., Monday to Friday)
www.lawyerlocator.co.uk
Provides details of lawyers, solicitors, barristers and advocates.

Resolution
Tel.: 01689 820272
www.resolution.org.uk

Mediation

www.advicenow.org.uk/family-mediation
An independent not-for-profit website providing advice on rights and legal issues for people in England and Wales: an information service brings together information from more than 200 UK websites.

Family Mediation Helpline
Tel.: 0845 60 26 627

MiD Mediation and Counselling (formerly **Mediation in Divorce**)
Tel.: 020 8891 6860
www.midmediation.org.uk/
Family mediation organization, covering south-west London and parts of Surrey, that helps those involved in family breakdown to communicate with one another and reach their own decisions on issues arising from separation or divorce.

Obtaining free advice

Citizens Advice (CAB)
For details of your local Citizens Advice Bureau, look in your local telephone directory or use a postcode search via the website.
www.citizensadvice.org.uk
www.adviceguide.org.uk

Divorce Aid
www.divorceaid.co.uk
This independent organization of professionals, based near Southport, aims to give advice, support and information on any matter concerning divorce.

www.wikivorce.com/divorce
Online provider of a wide range of information.

Protecting your home

Land Registry
Tel.: 020 7917 8888
www.landregistry.gov.uk
Land Registry keeps a register of title to freehold and leasehold land throughout England and Wales. Registering land helps to protect against fraud. Full details are set out in its 2008 Framework Document, which is available from the website.

3 Ending the relationship: your legal options

Civil partnerships

Stonewall
Information Line: 08000 50 20 20 (9.30 a.m. to 5.30 p.m., Monday to
Friday)
www.stonewall.org.uk

4 Decrees and orders of nullity

Forced marriage

The Foreign and Commonwealth Office Forced Marriage Unit
Tel.: 020 7008 0151 (general enquiries)
www.fco.gov.uk

Gender recognition

Gender Recognition Panel
www.grp.gov.uk/
The Panel assesses applications from transsexual people for legal
recognition of the gender in which they now live.

5 Property and financial matters

Bankruptcy

The Insolvency Service
Helpline: 0845 602 9848
www.insolvency.gov.uk

UK Insolvency Helpline
0800 074 6918
www.insolvencyhelpline.co.uk
A debt advice service for consumers and business.

Enforcement of court orders

Central Attachment of Earnings Payment System (CAPS)
PO Box 404
Northampton NN1 2ZY
Tel.: 01604 601555 (lines very busy between 10 a.m. and 2 p.m.)

Inheritance

Inheritance (Provision for Family and Dependants) Act 1975
Details may be downloaded from the following website:
www.opsi.gov.uk/acts/acts1975/pdf

Legal aid

Community Legal Advice
Helpline: 0845 345 4 345
www.communitylegaladvice.org.uk
Offers free, confidential and independent legal advice for residents of
England and Wales. A helpline site of the Legal Services Commission.

Legal Services Commission
www.legalservices.gov.uk

State benefits

Department of Work and Pensions
www.dwp.gov.uk
www.adviceguide.org.uk
Those without access to the internet can seek advice at their local Job
Centre or Job Centre Plus, or their local Citizens Advice Bureau.

6 Your children's best interests

Advice for parents

Parentline Plus
Helpline: 0808 800 2222 (free from landlines and most mobiles)
www.parentlineplus.org.uk
A national charity providing help and support for anyone caring for
children, whether parents, grandparents or step-parents.

Child abduction

Reunite International Child Abduction Centre
Tel.: 0116 2556 234 (advice line)
www.reunite.org

Child support

Child Maintenance Advice Centre
Tel.: 01207 693666 (confidential helpline)
http://childsupportadvice.co.uk
Deals with child support casework, advice and child-maintenance
tribunals.

Child Maintenance Options
Tel.: 0800 988 0988 (freephone)
www.cmoptions.org
Helps with understanding choices for arranging child maintenance in the UK.

Child Support Agency (CSA)
Tel.: 08457 133 133 (8 a.m. to 8 p.m., Monday to Friday; 9 a.m. to 5 p.m., Saturdays)
www.csa.gov.uk

Help for children
ChildLine
Tel.: 0800 1111
www.childline.org.uk

Parental alienation syndrome
Families Need Fathers
Helpline: 0300 0300 363
www.fnf.org.uk
Provides information and support to parents, including unmarried parents, helping fathers to know their rights as fathers; they believe children need both parents fully involved in their lives.

MATCH (Mothers Apart from Their Children)
www.matchmothers.org
www.dont-forget-about-daddy.co.uk

Single parents
Gingerbread
Tel.: 0808 802 0925 (helpline)
gingerbread.org.uk
A registered support charity run by lone parents for lone parents. The website includes links to regional groups.

Step-parents
www.beingastepparent.co.uk
This website provides online support and publishes a newsletter.

7 Your final hurdle: the legal process

List of courts for civil partners
- Birmingham
- Brighton
- Bristol
- Cardiff
- Chester
- Exeter
- Leeds
- Manchester
- Newcastle
- London – Principal Registry of the Family Division, London

Obtaining forms and information

Her Majesty's Courts Service (HMCS)
www.hmcourts-service.gov.uk
The website is an excellent source of information and forms which can be downloaded without charge.

Children and Family Court Advisory and Support Services (CAFCASS)
www.cafcass.gov.uk

8 Facing the future

Administrative matters

Driver and Vehicle Licensing Agency (DVLA)
Tel.: 0300 790 6801
www.dvla.gov.uk

General Register Office
www.gro.gov.uk/gro/content/certificates

TV Licensing
www.tvlicensing.co.uk

United Kingdom Identity and Passport Service
Tel.: 0300 222 0000 (Passport Advice Line)
www.ips.gov.uk

Dating

Association of British Introduction Agencies
Tel.: 020 8742 0386
www.abia.org.uk
The website includes details of the Code of Practice for online agencies.

Gray and Farrar
Tel.: 020 7290 9505
www.grayandfarrar.com
A prestigious introduction agency which takes exceptional care with its clients.

Education and retraining

Universities and Colleges Admissions Service
Tel.: 0871 468 0 468 (Customer Service Unit)
www.ucas.ac.uk
Provides details of further and higher education courses.

www.businesslink.gov.uk/bdotg/action/gsd
www.fundingeducation.co.uk/paying-your-tuition-fees.html
www.grantsforindividuals.org.uk
These websites provide a wide range of relevant information, including details of grants for education or for businesses.

Further reading

Abedin, Dr Humayra. 'I Can't Forgive or Forget What They Did to Me', *Independent*, 5 July 2009.

French, Alan and Carver, Jessica. *The Educational Grants Directory 2009–2010*. Directory of Social Change in association with Bates, Wells & Braithwaite, London, 2009.

Hollis, James. *Finding Meaning in the Second Half of Life*. Gotham Books, New York, 2005.

Kübler-Ross, Elisabeth and Kessler, David. *On Grief and Grieving: Finding the meaning of grief through the five stages of loss*. Simon and Schuster, New York, 2005.

Ruthven, Suzanne, Chapman, John and Langford, Polly. *Would Like to Meet: The dating game*. Ignotus Press, London, 2006, <www.ignotuspress.com>.

Trollope, Joanna. *Other People's Children*. Black Swan, London, 2008.

Welstead, Mary and Edwards, Lilian. *Family Law*, second edition (third edition will be published in 2011). Oxford University Press, Oxford, 2008; see Chapters 2 and 3 for validity of relationships, Chapter 4 for rights in the family home, Chapter 8 for inheritance.

Index